THE
GREAT COMPOSERS
THEIR LIVES AND TIMES

Baroque
Festival

Antonio
Vivaldi
1678-1741

George Frideric
Handel
1685-1759

Staff Credits

Editors
David Buxton BA (Honours)
Sue Lyon BA (Honours)

Art Editors
Debbie Jecock BA (Honours)
Ray Leaning BA (Honours),
PGCE (Art & Design)

Deputy Editor
Barbara Segall BA

Sub-editors
Geraldine Jones
Judy Oliver BA (Honours)
Nigel Rodgers BA (Honours), MA
Penny Smith
Will Steeds BA (Honours), MA

Designers
Steve Chilcott BA (Honours)
Shirin Patel BA (Honours)
Chris Rathbone

Picture Researchers
Georgina Barker
Julia Calloway BA (Honours)
Vanessa Cawley

Production Controllers
Sue Fuller
Steve Roberts

Secretary
Lynn Smail

Publisher
Terry Waters Grad IOP

Editorial Director
Maggi McCormick

Production Executive
Robert Paulley BSc

Managing Editor
Alan Ross BA (Honours)

Consultants
Dr Antony Hopkins
Commander of the Order
of the British Empire,
Fellow of the
Royal College of Music

Nick Mapstone BA (Honours), MA

Keith Shadwick BA (Honours)

Reference Edition Published 1990
Published by Marshall Cavendish Corporation
147 West Merrick Road
Freeport, Long Island
N.Y. 11520

Typeset by Walkergate Press Ltd, Hull, England
Printed and bound in Singapore by
Times Offset Private Ltd.

© *Marshall Cavendish Limited MCMLXXXIV,*
MCMLXXXVII, MCMXC
Library of Congress Cataloging-in-Publication Data

The Great composers, their lives and times.

Includes index.
· *1. Composers—Biography.   2. Music appreciation.*
I. Marshall Cavendish Corporation.
ML390.G82   1987   780'.92'2 [B]   86-31294
ISBN 0-86307-776-5

ISBN 0-86307-776-5 (set)
     0-86307-780-3 (vol)

THE
GREAT COMPOSERS
THEIR LIVES AND TIMES

Baroque
Festival

Antonio
Vivaldi
1678-1741

George Frideric
Handel
1685-1759

MARSHALL CAVENDISH
NEW YORK · LONDON · SYDNEY

THE
GREAT COMPOSERS
THEIR LIVES AND TIMES

Contents

Introduction

The term 'Baroque' is now used to describe European culture from the early-17th to the mid-18th centuries, but the word probably derives from the Portuguese, barocco, meaning a misshapen pearl, and was first used to describe an extremely ornamental style in art that began in Italy after 1600. As the style travelled north, it underwent many variations and the term becomes increasingly difficult to define, but the two main ingredients of the Baroque, at least in architecture and music, are complexity and harmony. Baroque composers used the characteristics of musical instruments in a new way; they were especially fond of the violin, which was perfected by the Amati, Stradivari and Guarneri families in Italy. The concerto was a favourite Baroque form, and in due course evolved into a sonata for several players. Later still, it developed into a form displaying the talents of a solo musician, thus achieving a greater contrast between the whole and its parts.

Vivaldi and Handel are generally recognized as the greatest exponents of the early- and mid-Baroque styles (Bach is the greatest composer of the late Baroque). There were, of course, other Baroque composers, who were once as famous as Vivaldi or Handel, but who are now largely forgotten. These composers are not only important for their part in the history of music and for their influence on the great composers (for example, Handel met Corelli in Italy), but also because their music is intensely enjoyable. Baroque music is increasingly popular and this volume provides the ideal introduction to its pleasures and complexities.

THE GREAT COMPOSERS

Music of the Baroque

A selection of composers: 1653 – 1767

Baroque composers like the Italians, Tomaso Albinoni and Arcangelo Corelli, the Germans, Johann Pachelbel and Georg Philipp Telemann, the Frenchman, Jean-Philippe Rameau and the Englishman, Henry Purcell, are now largely forgotten outside their own countries. Such neglect is unfortunate since each produced work of great originality and each was seen by his contemporaries as being a master of his art. The following pages redress the balance by examining the lives of these composers and, in the Listener's Guide, by analyzing some of their most important works. The age in which they lived was one of dynamic political, cultural and social change. As In the Background describes, the career of Charles II of England can be seen as a model for these changes. From being a virtual beggar at the courts of Europe, Charles, after the restoration of the monarchy, presided over a flowering of the arts in England after their suppression by the Puritan Commonwealth.

COMPOSER'S LIFE
'A Baroque ensemble'

Though the Baroque period is dominated by Vivaldi, Handel and Bach, the group of composers featured here did much to inspire and contribute to the spirit and style of the time.

Now sadly neglected, or much under-rated, composers such as the Italians Albinoni and Corelli, the Germans Pachelbel and Telemann, the Frenchman Rameau and the Englishman Purcell, were considered great musical exponents in their day. All were seen as geniuses in their chosen form of musical expression and the work of each of them was unique and original. Taken together they complete the picture of this period of musical grandeur and present a distinquished repertoire of the art of an age.

Because there are so many styles and such a variety of forms it is difficult to identify enough elements central to the work of all the composers to define, in simple terms, a 'Baroque school'. One common feature, however, is the continuo part (a part which provides a bass line, above which the melody instruments are free to produce their own lines), thus exploiting the potential of individual instruments such as the violin and the organ. Instrumental forms including the sonata and suite gained ground and were used with great imagination; opera became established as a genre and stylistic influences throughout Europe became common as a result of the boom in music publishing.

One of the main characteristics of Baroque music is the emphasis placed on virtuosity. Highlighting this was the development of instrumental forms, including the sonata and suite. String instruments, the violin in particular, were greatly favoured.

8

Tomaso Albinoni

Of all Baroque composers, Tomaso Giovanni Albinoni was perhaps the most personally independent and musically insular. Not tempted to seek a church or court post, Albinoni preferred to remain a *dilettante*. His encounters with other musicians were limited to being a kind of violin-playing overseer, and although he wrote a vast amount of music, it was predominantly vocal rather than instrumental.

Born in Venice on 14 June 1671, Albinoni was the son of a wealthy paper merchant and land and property owner. The names of his early teachers cannot be traced possibly because he was largely self-taught, for his first compositions were unsophisticated; and although he never achieved the profundity of Corelli or Vivaldi, he was ranked with them in popularity.

By his early twenties Albinoni's first sonatas had been published and his first opera, *Zenobia*, performed in his native city. Soon after 1700 other Italian cities began to show an interest in the operas he was by then turning out at a rate of one or two a year. A performance of his *Griselda* in 1703 took him to Florence to supervise the production and lead the orchestra. In 1705 Albinoni married an opera singer, Margherita Rimondi, who was 13 years his junior.

His father's death brought him back to Venice in 1709 where he inherited part of a considerable estate. But rather than taking on the responsibilities of the family business, Albinoni, now totally committed to music, opened a singing school with his wife as principal teacher.

By this time Albinoni's operas and concertos were becoming well known outside Italy, and his wife's operatic activities in Munich in 1721 probably helped to make his name known there. Albinoni dedicated a set of 12 concertos to Maximilian Emanuel II, Elector of Bavaria, and was promptly invited to Munich to supervise some of his own stage works. His wife's sudden death lead to the closing of the singing school—and the end of his ties to Italy. Thereafter his career took on a European flavour, and he spent the rest of his working life directing foreign performances of his operas. His composing activities decreased until 1741, when he retired. Albinoni died on 17 January 1751, aged 79.

Tomaso Giovanni Albinoni (above), one of the most prolific composers of the Baroque era, was a dilettante – a man of independent wealth who was able to pursue his own musical development and set his own level of involvement without the constraints of an employer or patron.

Albinoni's musical output was vast. He wrote 40 solo cantatas, 79 cantatas for mixed instruments, 59 concertos and 8 sinfonias, but in his day he was most acclaimed for his operas. He wrote at least 80 of them which were performed all over Italy in theatres like that shown below.

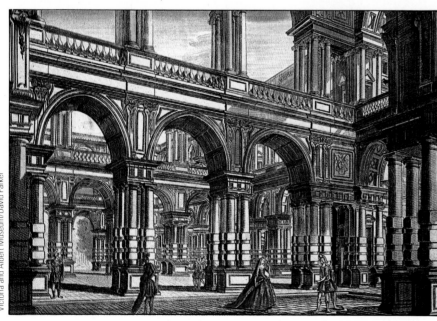

Johann Pachelbel

Less well-known now than other Baroque composers, Johann Pachelbel was in fact a major figure in his time. Fate dealt somewhat harshly with him and circumstances led to a restless mobility, but his output was prodigious and stamped with his unique imagination.

Born in the autumn of 1653 in Nuremburg, Pachelbel's early interest in music was nurtured by his family. After studying in his native city he was sent, at the age of 16, to Altdorf University, but despite securing a post as organist at the nearby church of St Lawrence, he had to leave university due to straitened family circumstances. He obtained a job as church organist of the Lorenzkirche – this brought in a mere pittance, but it gave Pachelbel more valuable experience.

In 1670 Pachelbel gained a place in the Gymnasium Poeticum at Regensburg, a classically-based grammar school founded by the city authorities in 1537. There he was regarded as an exceptionally gifted pupil: his refined manner and cultured background secured him a scholarship. Because his remarkable musical gifts were too advanced for the Gymnasium's facilities, he was given extramural training by Kaspar Prentz. In 1673 Pachelbel moved to Vienna where he came under the influence, if not under the actual tutorship, of Johann Kaspar Kerll, a notable composer who had taught Prentz. Pachelbel then obtained the post of deputy organist at St Stephen's Cathedral—one of the most famous and

The title page (right) from Pachelbel's Hexachordum Appollinis, *published in 1699, describes the work as a group of six arias with variations, which could be performed on the organ or harpsichord. The work is generally regarded as Pachelbel's major achievement as a composer of variations.*

The turmoil in European towns and villages, resulting from invasions by France and members of the Grand Alliance into each other's territory from 1689 to 1697, led to the displacement of many ordinary citizens (below). Pachelbel and his family fled from Stuttgart in 1692 to his home city of Nuremburg ahead of invading French troops.

By permission of the British Library

beautiful edifices in Europe.

In 1677 he left Vienna to take up a post as court organist at Eisenach in Thuringia, just inside the border of what is now East Germany. After a year he moved a little further east to become organist at the Predigerkirche in Erfurt, where he at last seemed content. He married Barbara Gabler, his first wife, and started a family; tragically he lost both his wife and son in the plague of 1683. A year later he married Judith Drommer: this was a happy, long-lasting and productive marriage that brought forth several gifted children, including two composers.

His 12 years at Erfurt were fruitful, though his job had one demeaning aspect: his contract specified that he had to submit to an annual examination to prove his musical progress, ability and taste; this took the form of a half hour recital of his own composition. This demand enabled him to become a first-rate composer for the organ.

While in Erfurt he was naturally drawn to the Bach family, and he became godfather to Ambrosius's daughter, Johanna Juditha. He also taught music to Johann Christoph (later known as the Ohrdruf Bach, and the teacher of the great Johann Sebastian).

In 1690 Pachelbel sought permission to leave his post to become musician and organist at the Württemburg court, Stuttgart. This appointment was short-lived: it was terminated when advancing French troops taking part against member countries of the Grand Alliance, forced him, along with much of the Stuttgart nobility, to flee eastward. Homeless, jobless and somewhat desperate, Pachelbel took his family to his home city of Nuremburg, where his Thuringian connections soon helped him to find employment as organist at Gotha, a town lying between Eisenach and Erfurt.

During his three years at Gotha he received invitations to fill organist posts at both Oxford and Stuttgart; he refused both but responded instead to an urgent plea from St Sebald's church in Nuremburg to fill the shoes of their recently deceased organist. He remained there until his death in March 1706.

Phillip Wouwermans 'The Sacking of a Village' Roy Miles Fine Paintings/Bridgeman Art Library

Georg Philipp Telemann

In an age of unbelievably prolific composers, Telemann stands out as by far the most productive. No composer before or since has approached his immense output: 30 operas, at least 100 oratorios, masses and other large-scale liturgical works, over 100 songs, more than 1350 cantatas, together with countless other vocal works for both sacred and secular occasions. And more: well over 100 orchestral suites, hundreds of chamber pieces for virtually every instrument current at the time, and many works for lute and keyboard instruments. He once admitted to feeling no particular affinity for the concerto form, so he completed only about 100 of them!

Telemann was born on 14 March 1681 in Nuremburg. Largely self-taught, he wrote his first opera at the age of 12. He entered Leipzig University as a law student — his parents forbade further musical involvement. However he was drawn into the Leipzig musical world when a room-mate secretly arranged to have one of his compositions performed at the Thomaskirche. From there his activities escalated — to the consternation of Kuhnau, head of the city's church music, on whose territory Telemann encroached. In 1705 Telemann left Leipzig and took up successive appointments at Sorau (where he married Louise Eberlin, who died in childbirth), Eisenach and Frankfurt (where he married Maria Katharina Textor).

On 16 October 1721 Telemann accepted the post of musical director of Hamburg's five main churches. The post demanded unprecedented productivity: he had to produce 100 cantatas per year, plus others for the frequent special occasions, in addition to a new passion and a new oratorio each year and music for every notable occasion in the calendars of all five churches.

On the secular side, Telemann was also asked to organise and provide music for public concerts and operatic productions in Hamburg, a task he undertook willingly and energetically without letting it interfere with his religious musical commitments.

Inevitably there was a clash of interests, with Hamburg's elders demanding that Telemann should not be allowed to perform secular music. Undaunted, Telemann simply applied for — and was accepted for — the post of Kantor at Thomaskirche, Leipzig, and duly filed his resignation. In reply to his act of bravado, the Hamburg authorities increased his salary and withdrew their objections to his work outside the churches; and the Leipzig appointment was awarded to Johann Sebastian Bach.

Vindicated, Telemann returned to his frenetic life in Hamburg. He became his own editor, manufacturer and sales department, in addition to engraving the plates from which the printing of his music was done. He had long intended to write books about musical theory, and from 1740 he tended to concentrate on this, though only slightly at the expense of his composing. In later life he produced a number of notable oratorios possibly influenced by Handel whom he had known since 1701 and whom he corresponded with regularly, and other works. He died in Hamburg on 25 June 1767 – his powers undiminished by over-use.

In an era when many composers were prolific in their musical output, Georg Philipp Telemann (above left), a largely self-taught composer and musician stands out as by far the most productive of all time. Regarded as Germany's leading composer of the early and mid-18th century, his work establishes him as the connecting link between the late Baroque and the new Classical styles.

In Hamburg from 1725 to 1740 Telemann was editor, manufacturer and distributor of his own publications, including a Song Book published in 1730 (left).

Rameau's most ambitious works are contained in his third collection of keyboard works. Described as 'character' pieces, and although inspired by everyday scenes of village and town life, like that shown left, they are musically dramatic. La poule (The Chicken), for instance, can be seen on one level as representational, but on another level is clearly a drama, with all the possible ranges of hope and despair.

Jean-Philippe Rameau

Rameau was one of the few native-born Baroque composers in France, but he would have been considered great in even a much more crowded field. Contemporary reports were unflattering: he was called mean with money and remote in manner in addition to being abnormally tall and thin 'with legs like flutes'. Fortunately he is judged today by his music, which is among the most charming and original of the Baroque era.

Born in Dijon in September 1683, he began composing while he was still at school. At university his musical interest took precedence over his legal studies, and he was asked to leave; with his parents' consent he spent a time in Milan as a music student.

A number of posts as church or cathedral organist followed: at Avignon, Clermont, Paris, Dijon (where he succeeded to his father's old post as church organist), Lyons and Clermont again. After seven years at Clermont, he devised a sly trick to escape from his contract. He was expected to play the organ at feast day in 1722 but he refused. Pressed, he commenced playing sulkily, and then he sprinkled more than a few wrong notes in his perfomance. The audience responded with consternation . . . and he was dismissed from his post.

Back in Paris he produced sketches and farces for Fair theatres and published two harpsichord books.

Jean-Philippe Rameau, one of the few native-born French Baroque composers produced some of the most charming and original music of the genre.

His finances improved, he married a girl 23 years his junior, Marie-Louise Mangot, who was a member of a prominent Lyons musical family. In 1732 he took a post as organist at Ste Croix-de-la-Bretonnerie where he enjoyed the patronage of Le Riche de la Poupelinière, a wealthy supporter of music, who introduced him to Voltaire and other writers.

Finding himself increasingly drawn towards dramatic music, he searched for a librettist; a year later, in 1733, the Abbé Pellégrin created a story, *Hippolyte et Aricie,* which he presented to Rameau. The cautious Abbé demanded a written guarantee against losses from this still little known composer, but at a preliminary rehearsal he was so delighted with the music that he tore up the guarantee.

The critics, however, detested Rameau's first opera, accusing him of writing in the Italian manner. Nevertheless the 'uneducated' audiences loved his music, and his career as an operatic composer was launched. Over the next 30 years he produced as many pieces of music designed for the theatre.

Rameau became involved in the absurd 'War of the Buffoons' which flared up in Paris in the 1750s between supporters of the French and the Italian opera styles. Ironically Rameau was accused of writing in the French manner by those very same commentators who had earlier accused him of writing Italian 'rubbish'.

In later years, when his creative powers waned, he said he regretted that he hadn't composed less and researched more into the principles of art. He died in Paris on 12 September 1764 of typhoid fever.

Arcangelo Corelli

When Corelli was born on 17 February 1653, his family was already rich and famous. Rich because of their productive estates around Fusignano in Italy. Famous because of the deeds of a relative, Rudolfo, who led a murderous attack upon a tyrannical overlord which almost attained success. As punishment Rudolfo was literally torn to pieces, the pieces were scattered round his house, the house was burned to the ground, the ground was flattened, ploughed, salted and flattened again, and a church was built on the spot. Atonement enough, evidently, for fate smiled on the family thereafter, and on Arcangelo Corelli in particular.

For Corelli – violinist, teacher, composer and director of musical ensembles – had the distinction of being first in a number of musical spheres: achieving fame exclusively from instrumental composition; building a reputation due to a boom in music publishing; and producing 'classic' instrumental works which were admired and imitated in his own time and in succeeding generations.

After early violin studies with a priest in the town of Faenza close to his home, Corelli moved to Bologna – in 1666 a musical centre of some consequence. There he was exposed to one of the most exciting musical environments that any young musician could wish for.

The huge church of S Petronio was the meeting place for a number of lively composers who used its two organs to support orchestras solely to fling musical phrases at each other across the echoing body of the church in a riot of competitive brilliance.

Although his musical output was modest, Arcangelo Corelli (below) exerted a strong influence on music both in his lifetime and after his death.

Unfortunately, there were no vacancies at S Petronio for the 17-year-old Corelli, and so instead he joined the Accademia Filarmonica as a violinist. This academy met at a private house and encouraged its members in all branches of music, including composition; such experience proved an invaluable aid to the budding young composer.

In 1675 Corelli moved to Rome. He started as a violinist in humble circumstances – having been recruited to play for a series of Easter oratorios, but his superb mastery of the instrument soon made him one of Rome's foremost players. On occasion he was also permitted to lead orchestras, and the skill he exhibited gave him considerable prominence and position.

Sir John Hawkins, who witnessed Corelli in action, gave an alarming picture of his demeanour when he was playing the violin: '. . . it was usual for his countenance to be distorted, his eyes to become as red as fire and his eyeballs to roll as in an agony.'

Another contemporary composer, Scarlatti, remarked on Corelli's discipline, the strictness of which was unique for his age. Scarlatti reported that he 'found nothing greatly to admire in (Corelli's) compositions, but he was struck by the manner in which he played his concertos and the nice management of his band, the uncommon accuracy of whose performance gave the concerts an amazing effect to the eye as well as to the ear. For Corelli regarded it as essential . . . that their bows should all move exactly together, all up, all down.' And if Corelli should find one unfortunate fiddler who was out of step with the rest, the whole performance was stopped and begun afresh.

Corelli enjoyed noble patronage almost from the start, including that of Queen Christina of Sweden to whom he dedicated his first opus, 12 trio sonatas. In 1684 he began to play regularly at functions organized by Cardinal Pamphili, whose Sunday academies were the focal point of Roman musical life. In 1687 he was appointed the cardinal's music master and was invited to live in his palazzo, together with Corelli's pupil and close friend, the violinist Matteo Fornari. During this period Corelli conducted orchestras of considerable size, and though it is possible that they were less brilliant, they were just as imposing as those at Bologna.

In 1690 Cardinal Pamphili moved to Bologna, but Corelli decided to remain in Rome. He was immediately taken up by the young Cardinal Pietro Ottoboni, nephew of Pope Alexander VIII; later Ottoboni would become influential in the careers of other great composers like Handel and Vivaldi. It was a most happy and fruitful time for Corelli. The Cardinal took a strong liking to his instrumental music, brought him to live with him in his palazzo and treated the composer more like a friend than an employee. The elevation of his status encouraged him to compose and it was during this time that his greatest works, his 12 *Concerti grossi,* were written. In 1706 he was admitted with Scarlatti to the Arcadian Academy, and the next year he met Handel and played uncharacteristically badly, according to reports, in Handel's *Il trionfo del tempo e del disinganno.* The following year he retired from public view, spending the last five years of his life revising his concerti grossi. He died on 8 January 1713, and was embalmed and buried in S Maria della Rotonda (the Pantheon); for several years afterwards the anniversary of his death was marked there by solemn performances of his concertos.

Henry Purcell

Henry Purcell was one of the greatest and most important composers in the Baroque period and in the history of English music.

When Purcell was born in London sometime during 1659 (the exact date is not known), the Baroque era was yet to attain its peak of achievement in the music of composers such as Bach and Handel, but the influence of Purcell on English music was as powerful and far-reaching on these and other composers.

Purcell's early death left a great void since there was a lack of strong native composers able to maintain the lines of musical development that Purcell had begun.

The son of a singer and composer, and therefore exposed to music from his earliest years, Purcell began composing when he was still a child. When he was only eight years old the precocious Purcell wrote a song which was published in Playford's *Catch that Catch Can, or The Musical Companion*. At this time Purcell was a chorister in the Chapel Royal. Evidently nothing interested him but music, and when his voice broke earlier than is usual, and the choir no longer had any use for him, he was content to assist, without pay, as the assistant to the keeper of the royal instruments, John Hingeston. Purcell clearly felt that it was far better to polish oboes and tune harpsichords than to devote himself to a trade that had no connection whatsoever with his beloved music.

Henry Purcell (above), one of the most important composers of the Baroque period and the history of English music, succeeded John Blow as organist at Westminster Abbey (left). The post entitled him to a salary and the rent of a house in St Ann's Lane, Westminster. He lived there until his death in 1695. His funeral took place in Westminster Abbey and he was buried in the north aisle. The burial place is marked by a marble plaque which can still be seen.

His persistence paid off, and within a year he was appointed to the slightly more elevated position of organ tuner and music copyist at Westminster Abbey. Then, upon the death of Matthew Locke in 1677, Purcell was made Composer-in-Ordinary.

In this capacity Purcell was expected to compose anthems and songs, plus instrumental music for the royal band of violins; unfortunately little of his music survives from this period.

Two years later, however, when he was 20, Purcell became the chief organist at Westminster Abbey. This position gave him a position of considerable security: not only did he receive a comfortable salary for that time, but also he was given a rent-free house near to the Abbey. A year later he married. Of his two surviving children, one, Edward, himself became an organist and composer.

The next few years in Purcell's life saw a dramatic increase in his musical activities, for further appointments were put upon his shoulders by the King, then Charles II; these were duly confirmed by the successive monarchs James II and William III and Mary. The most important of these appointments was that of organ maker and keeper of the king's instruments. Purcell succeeded John Hingeston in this post when Hingeston died in 1683. Earlier in that year Purcell published his *Sonnata's of III Parts,* which were dedicated to Charles II.

During this time Purcell's music widened and deepened both in quality and in quantity. He produced chamber music, incidental music for stage works, odes and songs, in additon to the services and semi-religious anthems that were expected of the most prominent church composer in the country.

It is possible to surmise that the arduous duties piled on Purcell eventually took their toll of his health, unlike Telemann who appeared to thrive – and indeed live to the great age of 86 – on the ever increasing pressure of musical composition.

All religious and state occasions, both large and small, important dates, ceremonies and other public events, had to be marked by fresh compositions; the king's violins had to be kept supplied with new music; and there was a constant pressing demand for the latest songs from his pen.

In all, Purcell provided music for more than 50 stage plays, operas and other dramatic productions, and he still found the time to compose a number of harpsichord pieces. These comprise suites and dances which may have been intended largely for use in his own home since they include a high proportion of arrangements made for the keyboard from stage works. Some of these suites and dances were published by Purcell's widow shortly after his death. The last royal occasion for which Purcell supplied music was the funeral of Queen Mary in 1694, the year before his own death.

In addition to all this, Purcell was still responsible for the upkeep of the king's instruments and, apparently, for the actual construction of organs; this was to become the cause of some financial dispute with the dean and chapter of Westminster Abbey, and eventually he was recompensed for his work.

Purcell died quite suddenly in November 1695 – no record exists of what illness befell him. Purcell made his will on the day of his death, but apparently he was so enfeebled by illness that he was unable to write it out. He received a fittingly grand funeral in Westminster Abbey on 26 November 1695, and he was buried in the north aisle, near the organ. The position is marked by a marble plaque, paid for by Lady Elizabeth Howard, and can still be seen today.

No reports of Purcell's character have survived. The few contemporary portraits show a man of mild-mannered expression, wide-eyed, noble-browed and with an equable air.

It is obvious from the scale and nature of his music, however, that he was deeply intelligent, hardworking and reliable, and capable of producing all kinds of the required music on time; yet he had a spark of adventurousness that led him to experiment with musical effects as, for instance, when he commenced an orchestral piece in a stage work with a drum solo. Such daring at the time must have had a profoundly shocking effect on Purcell's listeners.

In 17th-century England it was considered wise for a composer to affect Italian taste. In one of his prefaces Purcell remarked: 'I have faithfully endeavour'd a just imitation of the most fam'd Italian masters.' This is nothing more than misleading modesty, for Purcell can never be accused of imitation; he was instead quite unique. In fact, the greatest Italian composer of the time, Arcangelo Corelli, could detect no Italian influence whatsoever in Purcell's music. On the other hand, some French influence may be found, but it is virtually hidden by Purcell's own skill and originality.

It was not until 15 years after Purcell's death, when George Frideric Handel (pages 57–100) arrived on the English musical scene from Germany, that the void that could not be filled by English musicians was finally occupied.

Handel's popularity as an English composer of oratorios sometimes obscures his position as one of the greatest exponents of the Baroque style of music.

A Baroque festival

The spirit and range of Baroque music is encapsulated in this selection of pieces which represent some of the greatest of its musical achievements.

What makes a piece of music popular? It may be an irresistible melody, like a Schubert song which instantly lodges itself in the listener's mind, or the hypnotic rhythm of, say, Ravel's *Bolero*. Or perhaps it is the grandeur of an orchestral texture, as in some romantic masterpieces or the tiny, balanced simplicity of a Renaissance madrigal. In most cases, it is probably a combination of all these things – rhythm, harmony, melody, overall shape and emotional content – plus an intangible element which adds its own unique appeal.

The ingredients that make a piece of Baroque music popular in the 20th century are undoubtedly different from those which appealed to the tastes of an 18th century audience. Many of Handel's great operas were opening-night disasters for example, and the music of J. S. Bach, which now resounds through our concert halls to great acclaim, was scorned in his own day as being over-complex and out-

dated. In fact, the most published piece of music in the 18th century was the *Stabat Mater* by Pergolesi – a sacred work which enjoys only modest success today and is rarely mentioned in anyone's top ten pieces of the century!

Overall, however, many Baroque compositions have become outstandingly popular in our time, thanks to a remarkable revival of interest in 18th century music. It seems to exude a serenity and positive belief in the future which is both powerfully magnetic and somehow comforting at times when our own age seems confused and unsettled. No doubt future historians will analyze our interest in such music, the pushing of our musical frontiers beyond the staple diets of the Classical and Romantic repertory, and will find some deep-rooted reason for the phenomenon; but for us it remains simply to enjoy the music of the Baroque era.

The selection that follows includes

The same sense of occasion and the supreme self-confidence that flows from Baroque music seems to fill the very air in the al fresco festival scene above.

some pieces which did not exist in their present form 200 years ago, but have been pieced together from fragments of manuscript or lifted out of their original context and given an 'up-to-date' treatment. Only the Corelli Concerto Grosso op. 6 No. 8 was as much a celebrated work in the composer's lifetime as it is today. Quite why the remainder have become so popular is difficult to say; it may be due to the good fortune that performers chose to play them or that the record industry chose to record them. Whatever the reason, they all help to illuminate a corner of that remarkable musical world we call the Baroque; a world whose style, self-assurance and rich expression have such strong appeal to modern audiences.

Purcell: Trumpet Overture from *The Indian Queen*

Imagine Drury Lane Theatre, London, in the year 1695. On stage is an extraordinary entertainment, not quite an opera yet more than a play. It is what the writer Roger North has dubbed a 'semi-opera'. The great drama of *The Indian Queen,* a play written in 1664 by John Dryden and Sir Robert Howard, had been transformed with music and song by Henry Purcell, then the recently deceased organist of Westminster Abbey. The background of the story is a war between Peru and Mexico, with appearances by the exotic King Montezuma and the priest-magician Ismeron.

In the first act there is no added music, but the second is introduced by a splendid 'symphony', followed by a masque. Then comes the third act, the climax of the drama. In a great incantation scene, Ismeron seeks to interpret a dream, in the song 'Ye twice ten hundred Deities'. But the God of Dreams appears and warns the people gathered 'Seek not to know what must not be revealed'. At this point, the sound of a trumpet overture breaks upon the scene and from this Purcell develops one of his finest instrumental pieces.

There are three sections in his short but magnificent Overture (originally, the word did not necessarily mean something that came at the start of an opera or instrumental suite – Purcell often used more than one, each at the start of a self-contained piece of music). The opening, a majestic movement, gives the trumpet martial dotted rhythms which are then taken up in the striding bass line. This leads into what Purcell calls a Canzona, that is, a fugal-style fast movement in which the parts enter one after another with bright, imitative music: the trumpet then returns to add its own imitative flourishes to the whole. After a development of these themes, the trumpet makes its final grand statement, before the music unexpectedly moves into a contrasting, slower tempo. The strings alone play a sequence of eloquent, noble harmonies which move gently towards the climax. The trumpet is silent as the music subsides and the major key of D is finally heard after the strings' more melancholy touch of D minor.

Albinoni/Giazotto: Adagio for strings and organ in G minor

There can be few examples of the modern Baroque revival that are more interesting than this short piece. Even though it seems quintessentially Baroque, it is entirely a creation of the 20th century.

Albinoni, who lived from 1671 to 1751, left many published works that were performed in his day, as well as uncompleted manuscripts that were never played. In 1945, the Italian scholar Remo Giazotto compiled a catalogue of Albinoni's works and shortly afterwards was sent some fragments of manuscript that had been

found in Dresden. These fragments included a bass line and two sections of a violin line – perhaps for a trio sonata movement.

Example 1

Giazotto thought them so memorable that, instead of just filing them away, he elaborated them into a complete movement.

The result is a piece of music far more redolent of the Romantic era than of the Baroque, though it retains something of a period 'feel'. Giazotto wrote out an organ part for the bass line (giving it a religious flavour the original would not have had). He also wrote gorgeous inner parts to accompany Albinoni's violin line, which are not true recreations of the Baroque era – rather, they are imaginative and skilful additions to the texture.

Giazotto cast the movement in three-part form. First, the melody is developed over a pulsating bass line and organ accompaniment. The central section which follows is a most unusual and highly effective series of cadenzas for solo instruments over organ chords. Then the regular rhythm returns and the opening piece is heard again, rising to a rich and heartfelt climax at the close.

Albinoni would probably have been delighted with this 20th-century arrangement.

G. Tiepolo 'America' (detail) Würrzburg Residenz/Scala

Rubens 'An Autumn Landscape with a View of Het Steen' (detail) The National Gallery, London

A sumptuous reminder of the exotic background to Purcell's semi-opera, The Indian Queen, *is provided by Tiepolo's allegorical painting* America *(left).*

The wistful beauty of Albinoni's Adagio *and the tragic death of Ophelia, as painted by Millais (right), share a timeless, haunting quality.*

Telemann: Viola Concerto in G

Telemann was an enormously prolific German composer whose reputation suffered at the hands of history; in the 19th century especially, he was unfavourably compared with his contemporary, J. S. Bach, and treated as a composer of quantity rather than quality. In the 18th century, however, Telemann was far more appreciated, both because he could write promptly and efficiently for any occasion and because his music has a flexible, fashionable style. He also cultivated a lighter style which was more typical of the rococo and galant music favoured in the mid-decades of the 18th century.

His earlier works are less experimental and very much in the traditional mould of the Baroque concerto, as established by Corelli. But Telemann's inexhaustible spirit of adventure found an outlet in writing music for unusual instruments. It is certainly a delightful surprise to find a concerto for viola dating from this period. The instrument was little favoured by composers and its role was regarded as no more than a filling out of orchestral texture in the middle range, usually accompanied by the keyboard continuo instrument. The viola did not become important in its own right until continuo passed from fashion and composers from the Classical era

The warm, autumnal textures of this landscape by Rubens (left), with its richness of detail and its expansive, early morning vistas, echo perfectly the changing moods of Telemann's masterly Viola Concerto in G.

In spite of its cheerful musical mimicry, the work is not simply a frivolous piece of fun; it is one of the composer's most powerfully-written essays. The theme has a biting insistence that Rameau's biographer describes as 'a drama with alternations of hope and despair'. The original motif is presented in various forms and so skilfully rearranged in the second half that the technical facility of the construction is perfectly disguised. However powerful the music becomes,

wrote equally for all four instruments of the string quartet. Telemann was, therefore, well ahead of his time when he wrote a piece to display the singularly mellow quality of the instrument – a piece that remains the premier solo viola concerto in the regular repertory.

Telemann's Concerto is in the slow-fast, slow-fast form of the church sonata, or *sonata da chiesa* (a term which distinguishes it from the *sonata da camera,* based on the form of the dance suite), often followed by Corelli in his concerto. The opening movement is broad, serene and calm, with an expansive, singing theme for the viola and an unobtrusive dotted rhythm which impels the music forward. It leads to the first and typically Baroque Allegro. The rising arpeggio, or chord figure, of the opening was a pattern used countless times by Baroque composers, but Telemann gives it a haunting insistence by holding the top note across the beat in rhythmic suspension. There then follows another supremely Baroque developmental idea, a sequence in which the same gesture is repeated several times at different pitches and is rounded off by a beautifully measured cadence. The soloist takes up the theme and develops it before the movement returns to the opening sequence and comes to its evocative close.

The second slow movement starts with answering pairs of phrases using just one small motif; the soloist enters without a bass line or continuo support but a single line of strings gives an ethereal, weightless quality to the music. The final, fast movement, as if to complement the first, has a descending scale figure in place of the rising arpeggio. The central note is emphasized by the cadence-type gesture

While Rameau's delightful parody of clucking hens in La poule *is mirrored in the farmyard scene (above), the underlying seriousness of the work is more effectively implied by the frontispiece to his composition (above right).*

with which the movement starts, but then the scale passage leads to another lively sequential development which the soloist takes up with verve.

Rameau: *La poule*

We have visited England, Italy and Germany in this sequence of Baroque works, and now it is the turn of France. Her genius, in the period of high Baroque, lay not in short orchestral pieces but in the writing of small 'character' pieces for either keyboard or ensemble. For this reason, *La poule* (the chicken), by Jean-Philippe Rameau, was originally composed for keyboard and is just one of many pieces he gave colourful titles to – though this is more deliciously descriptive of the music than most.

It appeared in Rameau's *Nouvelles Suites de Pièces de Clavecin,* published in Paris around 1728. The piece bears the literal verbal rendering of the musical opening 'Co co co co co co co dai', and the resemblance to the clucking of a hen needs no further emphasis.

Example 2

There also survives an arrangement of *La poule* for chamber ensemble, which is not by Rameau but does provide the basis for the present transcription for chamber orchestra.

the clucking recurs with considerable force and the moment when the bass pounds the theme down to the bottom of its range is quite remarkably fierce. Such force shows how misleading it is to think of French Baroque music as being merely decorative and artificial; Rameau not only provides touches of light-hearted entertainment but also reaches great depths of emotional expression.

Pachelbel: Canon and Gigue

This is another Baroque work which owes its present fame to modern arrangements. In its original form, Pachelbel's little Canon was a piece for three solo violins and continuo. Unfortunately, it does not survive as an original manuscript and we cannot be certain that it was composed by Pachelbel. Even so, his style, with its distinctively rich North German texture, is accurately reflected.

The work is most usually played by a chamber orchestra – with double basses to give extra weight and substance to the hypnotic ground bass pattern that is heard throughout.

Example 3

The Canon is constructed so that each of the three upper parts play the same line in turn. The effect, a gradual build up of mesmerising tension, is quite unlike anything found elsewhere in Baroque music, which more typically depends on the alternating rise and fall of tension and relaxation. With 28 repetitions of its ground bass, Pachelbel's Canon is more like a Baroque version of Ravel's *Bolero*.

In the earliest manuscript copy, the work is paired with a little Gigue, also for three violins and continuo, which provides light relief after the serious mood of the canon. It is often left out of modern arrangements, thus distorting the mood, but here is included in a complementary version for chamber orchestra.

Corelli: Concerto Grosso in G minor Op 6 No. 8 (Fatto per la notte di Natale)

This superb Concerto was highly praised as a model of its kind in the 18th century

and its fame has endured to this day. The historian Charles Burney wrote with enthusiasm that 'the harmony is so pure, so rich and so graceful; the parts are so clearly, judiciously and ingeniously disposed; and the effect of the whole, from a large band, so majestic, solemn and sublime, that they preclude all criticism, and make us forget that there is any other music of the same kind existing'.

The Concerto, published in Amsterdam in 1714, follows the slow-fast, slow-fast sequence of the church sonata – but with some important additions. After the initial chordal flourish, a slow, eloquent Grave unfolds imitatively; the composer himself has added the instruction *'Arcate sostenuto e come sta'* (sustained bowing; play it as written – that is, without ornamentation). The first Allegro places suspensions over a rapidly moving bass line; here a solo group of two violins and cello stand out from the full orchestra. The

With all the weighty atmosphere of a state procession (below), Pachelbel's Canon moves forward with slow and solemn deliberation.

F. Guardi 'Papal Visit in Venice' (detail). The Cleveland Museum, Gift of the Hanna Fund

Understanding music: how the orchestra began

Right up to the late Renaissance period around the mid-1500s, instrumental music had always played a subservient role as the accompaniment to singers or dancers: in fact, the word orchestra in ancient Greek drama referred to the circular space in front of the stage in which the dance or *orchesis,* was performed by the chorus. However, by the time of the early Baroque period, composers had gradually begun to write independent instrumental music. One of the pioneers of this breakaway tendency was the Venetian composer Giovanni Gabrieli (1554–1612). In his secular sonatas for wind instruments, the sounds produced by the specific instruments were deliberately contrasted as in the vocal polyphony of the time. Monteverdi further developed this idea in his opera, *La Favola d'Orfeo,* produced in Mantua in 1607. Though the orchestra chosen to accompany the singers was still basically a Renaissance chamber group, he selected the component instruments with great care in order to highlight the contrast in tone colour, range and dynamics.

Jean Baptiste Lully (1632–87) who directed the court musicians of Louis XIV, made further advances in orchestral style and technique. His orchestra, *Les vingt-quatre violons du Roy,* was frequently supplemented by players from the *Grande Ecurie,* a woodwind band used for military music.

By the early 1700s, new instruments were introduced and old favourites were being steadily improved — the more extrovert violins ousted the old viols and the primitive hunting horn evolved into a more playable musical instrument.

The Baroque period reached its climax with Johann Sebastian Bach. Bach gloried in instrumental technique but was hampered throughout his working life by a deficiency of well-trained musicians. His strongly contrapuntal outlook produced strands of interweaving melody of almost equal importance, with a continuo player at the keyboard filling in the lower harmonies.

Handel, on the other hand, had fairly large, fully professional orchestras at his disposal. At the peak of his career, he could command striking dramatic effects with a combination of twelve violins, three violas, three cellos, two basses, four oboes, two trumpets, two horns and percussion.

The most far-reaching influence on the development of the orchestra during the beginning of the Classical period was exerted by a group of expert composer-musicians at the court of the Elector Karl Theodor at Mannheim. They were directed by the brilliant virtuoso violinist, Johann Stamitz (1717–57). The group became famous throughout Europe for its controlled, accurate and sensitive playing and for the elevation of the violins ·to the leading role. Europe's musicians came, saw and were conquered at Mannheim, returning home determined to emulate this new style of ensemble playing.

The orchestra became more or less standardized by the time of Haydn and Mozart. This was to no small extent due to the popularity of their work all over Europe which necessitated the correct number of musicians performing their work anywhere. The keyboard no longer formed part of the orchestra and though wind instruments were not perceptibly increased, the string sections were heavily reinforced, while percussion was still largely restricted to timpani.

It was very much this organized body of musicians that Beethoven inherited: an orchestra which required music composed for it as a whole, exploiting its various timbres and sonorities within the unity of the sonata form, rather than pitting the various forces against each other as Baroque ensembles had done earlier. Beethoven fully realized the untapped potential of this: in his Symphony No. 1 in C, the rumbles of this revolutionary approach can be heard, challenging the last echoes of Classicism. Music would never sound the same again.

Many Baroque instrumental ensembles consisted of string and wind combinations such as that of the viol and transverse flutes (left).

Corelli's **Pastorale** *(above) seems to anticipate the mysticism of Handel's chorus* **Glory to God** *and, as the music fades, it too leaves an ethereal image of angels returning to heaven (right).*

second slow movement, marked Adagio, has rippling arpeggios for the small group of soloists and leads straight into a central Allegro, a brilliant movement in which harmony and rhythm are paramount. The Adagio then returns to be followed by a *Vivace* in the style of a minuet and an Allegro in the form of a gavotte. Both feature the solo group and allow the full band to join in and reinforce the cadences.

The Concerto's most famous movement, a *Pastorale* (a piece traditionally played on Christmas morning) comes last. It is marked 'ad libitum', which seems to imply that, up to this point, the piece could be played at any time in the year, while the *Pastorale* would be added only for Christmas day. This device puts the work in line with concertos like those composed by Giuseppe Torelli, Francesco Manfredini and the Pifa, or Pastoral Symphony, in Handel's *Messiah.* The characteristics of all these pieces are simple, drone-line accompaniments and a swinging rhythm of 12 quavers in the bar (four groups of

Example 4

three). Corelli's piece is, however, an especially eloquent example of the genre. It dies away at the close to an exquisite *pianissimo* (very quiet), as if portraying the angels disappearing through the gates of heaven.

Detail from The Wilton Diptych. The National Gallery, London

Handel: Sinfonia to Act III, *Solomon: Arrival of the Queen of Sheba*

Handel's great oratorios contain many fine instrumental numbers and interludes, notably the sinfonias that introduce an act or part of the work. Justly famous among them is this exhilarating introduction to Act III of the oratorio, *Solomon*. The whole work was composed with typical virtuosity, between 5 May and 13 June 1748, yet is one of Handel's richest and most effective works. It was first heard at Covent Garden in March 1749, where it was given 'after the manner of an oratorio', that is, without any staging. The story of Solomon was adapted from Old Testament sources by an anonymous librettist who probably worked closely under the composer's direction.

It is not clear where the familiar title, *Arrival of the Queen of Sheba,* originated: the scintillating music of the sinfonia is usually performed with such speed and brilliance that it seems ill-suited to the mood required for the grandiose entrance of a queen – even one as racy as the Queen of Sheba! Instead, the music provides a hectic, bustling theme for the orchestra, combining arpeggios with a rushing downward scale that returns in various guises and keys and is contrasted with a perky theme for two solo oboes. Perhaps, as Winton Dean suggests, the idea is not to portray the queen's actual entrance, but the frantic preparations for her impending visit at the court of King Solomon.

Other well-known pieces by Handel include the magnificent *Messiah* (pages 75–83), and his works for great outdoor occasions – *Music for the Royal Fireworks* and *Water Music* (pages 84–91).

Though Solomon *(below) and many other Handel oratorios are seldom played today, this exquisite music was much admired by his contemporaries.*

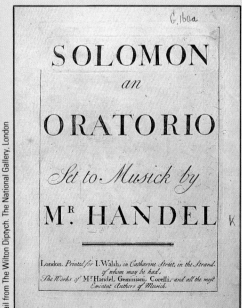

G. 1600

SOLOMON
an
ORATORIO
Set to Musick by
M.ʳ HANDEL

London. *Printed for* I. Walsh, *in Catharine Street, in the Strand. of whom may be had,* The Works of M.ʳ Handel, Geminiani, Corelli, *and all the most Eminent Authors of Musick.*

By permission of the British Library

Great interpreters

The distinguished Italian ensemble, I Musici (right), has a particular enthusiasm for Baroque music, and gave its first recital in 1952. The group has travelled widely, and perform works by many Baroque composers including Vivaldi, Torelli and Gabrieli. For more information on I Musici, see page 48.

Mike Evans

FURTHER LISTENING

Henry Purcell
1. Dido and Aeneas – Opera (1689)
2. The Fairy Queen – Pastiche (1692)
3. Ode on St Cecilia's Day (1692)

Tomaso Albinoni
1. 12 Concerti a Cinque, op. 9 (1722)
2. 12 Concerti a Cinque, op. 7 (1716)
3. Pimpinone – Opera (1708)

Georg Philipp Telemann
1. Musique de Table (Tafelmusik)
2. The 'Paris' Quartets, Nos. 1–9
3. St Mark Passion (1759)

Jean-Philippe Rameau
1. Pièces de Clavecin, Livre I
2. Les Indes Galantes – Ballet Suite
3. Castor et Pollux – Opera (1737)

Johann Pachelbel
1. Harpsichord Works
2. Chaconne in F minor
3. Suite in G for Strings & Continuo

Arcangelo Corelli
1. 12 Sonatas for Violin & Continuo op. 5
2. 12 Concerti Grossi, op. 6 (1714)

Other Composers of Interest:

Claudio Monteverdi (1567–1643)
Although preceding the Baroque era, Monteverdi is of enormous significance in the development of both opera and non-stage vocal works. His music is marked by strongly coloured harmony and melodic sweetness and beauty. His operas, such as *Orfeo, L'Incoronazione di Poppaea,* and *Il Ritorno d'Ulisse,* have enjoyed a recent revival of popularity, and are quite worthy of it. His *Madrigals of Love and War* are an important collection, in terms of influence and their own worth. His *Vespro della Beata Vergine (1610)* is an undoubted masterpiece.

Christoph Willibald Gluck (1714–1787)
Gluck's name will be forever associated with the reform of opera he and his colleagues set out to achieve by writing such works as *Orpheé and Euridice* and *Alceste.* It is the former work which keeps his name alive for modern audiences, and indeed that work displays all the merits he was anxious to achieve for opera – a coherent plot; music no longer at the service of the virtuoso vocalist; recitative and accompanied arias integrated with dramatic unity. Gluck was a powerful composer of considerable dramatic impact, and it is as such, and as the composer of the memorable arias contained in his operas, that he is revered today. Gluck wrote a great many operas during his lifetime, both in the old and 'reformed' style, and also completed a quantity of ballet and instrumental music, though it is only through his handful of truly great operas that his reputation has been sustained.

Domenico Scarlatti (1685–1757)
Son of the composer Alessandro Scarlatti (1660–1725), Domenico was in his lifetime recognised as a supremely gifted virtuoso of the harpsichord, and he wrote over 500 sonatas for his favourite instrument. These one-movement sonatas show an astonishing variety in mood, texture and sound, especially considering the relative inflexibility of the instrument they were written for. Scarlatti was also very active in the vocal field, producing a great deal of church music, including a fine *Stabat Mater,* and about twelve operas which have fallen into subsequent obscurity.

Marc-Antoine Charpentier (?1645–1704)
Charpentier, along with Lully and the slightly later Francois Couperin, is a good illustration of the development of music in France as opposed to Germany or Italy during the formative years of Baroque. He worked, as did Lully, in conjunction with the great Molière, writing incidental music for the dramatist's last play, but it is in his sacred music that we find his greatest achievement. The oratorio *Judith* is a triumphant piece of choral writing, possessing great power in its solo items as well as the unison passages. The three volume of *Leçons de Tenèbres* are full of moments of great beauty, as are other sacred pieces such as the beautiful *Pastorale,* the *Te Deum* and both *Magnificats.*

John Dowland (1563–1626)
Dowland, like Monteverdi, falls outside the immediate chronology of this volume, but should not be overlooked. A key figure, along with Byrd and Morley, in the astonishing English Renaissance of the later Tudor years, he composed a great quantity of songs and lute music – pavanes, galliards and so forth – which in retrospect stand as the greatest of their time. He completed four *Bookes of Songs* between 1597 and 1612, the last of which carries the title *A Pilgrimes Solace,* and these are masterful achievements, full of endlessly inventive melodies and harmonic accompaniments. The pervading air of his work as a whole is one of deep and passionate melancholy.

IN THE BACKGROUND
'The merry monarch'

After the grey days of Puritanism the restoration of the king – Charles II – injected dull England with a new vitality, promoting writers, dramatists and musicians to revive their long-suppressed talents.

On May 25th, 1660 Charles Stuart and his court landed at Dover. It had been nine years since the Prince made his dramatic escape to exile, disguised as a serving maid, and eleven years since the execution of his father Charles I. The Civil War and the Puritan Government of Oliver Cromwell's Commonwealth had dominated England since 1642. But Cromwell's death left a gap in the government of the nation which his son Richard could not fill. So at the invitation of parliament and to great popular acclaim, Charles returned to take the throne.

Tears were shed as the King was welcomed ashore by leading nobles and gentry before a large gathering of local people. All the way to London, the route was lined with cheering crowds. The new king symbolized an end to the grey, austere and lacklustre Puritanism. Here was a handsome man, splendidly attired, well known for his love of mirth, pretty women, wagers and wine. On May 1st the people had thronged to the Maypoles for the traditional dancing that had been banned under the Commonwealth. Now they came out to greet Charles II – the 'Merry Monarch'.

Oliver Cromwell became Lord Protector of England in 1653. With the help of his strait-laced parliament he ruled the Commonwealth with a rod of iron until his death in 1658. The Dunbar medal (right and below) commemorated Cromwell's victory over Charles at the famous Battle of Dunbar in 1650.

Tired of the drab restrictive life-style imposed upon them by the Puritans, the people of England welcomed their 'Merry Monarch', Charles II (right), with open arms. His philosophy that 'God will never damn a man for allowing himself a little pleasure' came like a breath of fresh air.

After nearly a decade of living in exile, Charles II was proclaimed king. The coronation procession from the Tower to Westminster (right) took place on April 23rd 1661 amid great rejoicing and festivity.

Dirk Stoop 'Coronation Procession of Charles II' Museum of London

Wily operator or puppet king?

Despite the wave of royalist feeling that brought Charles II to the throne, he was not to enjoy unlimited freedom. Charles came back on conditions that were set by parliament and placed very definite constraints on his actions. Under the Commonwealth most of the crown lands had been sold and feudal tenure abolished so that the monarch was now to be dependent on parliament for his money supply. The Restoration brought with it a sense of relief – the period of change and uncertainty, of turmoil and in-fighting was ended – and this was without doubt heightened by the knowledge that the powers of the

Catholic alike, from any positions of power or responsibility in the country. And Charles' financial dependence on parliament made it very difficult for him to go against their wishes. The distinctive feature of his reign, therefore, was his wily manoeuvring to bypass the obstruction of parliament without provoking serious antagonisms.

The religious question also entered into foreign policy during this time. The English were intermittently at war with protestant Holland over conflicting trading interests, and in 1667 the Dutch scored a decisive victory when their fleet sailed right up the Thames to set fire to the English ships in the

Religious differences featured strongly throughout Charles' reign. Anti-Catholic fervour soared in 1678 with the discovery of a conspiracy to kill the king and place his brother James on the throne. Titus Oates became a national hero for uncovering the 'Popish Plot', until it became clear that it was a large-scale fabrication. Oates was found guilty of perjury, put in the pillory (right), flogged and imprisoned.

Museum of London

King were now restricted, and the hope that parliament and the sovereign could now rule together for the good of England.

In theory the notion of 'constitutional monarchy' was the perfect solution, but in practice events proved rather more complex. The religious controversy between the Protestant and the Roman Catholic churches that had culminated in civil war continued to dominate English politics right through Charles' reign. Although Charles II was known to have Catholic sympathies he was overruled by the staunchly Anglican parliament which passed laws to exclude dissenters, both Protestant and Roman

Jan Vorsterman 'Greenwich from One Tree Hill'. The National Maritime Museum, London

from 1672 to 1674. In return he secured a handsome subsidy from Louis which for a while freed him from the constraints of parliament. However, in 1674 when it became clear that the French were not succeeding in conquering the Dutch, Charles pulled out of the alliance and made his peace with the Dutch. Anglo-Dutch relations were further improved and an alliance cemented with the marriage of Charles' niece Mary, Protestant daughter of James and heir to the throne, to William of Orange in 1677. From their Dutch court this devout couple took a careful interest in developments in England, concerned both for the future of their faith and for the security of what was eventually to become their crown.

The following year a torrent of anti-papist sentiment swept through England with the discovery of the 'Popish Plot' – a fabricated Roman Catholic conspiracy 'invented' by Titus Oates. Anyone suspected of having connections with the church of Rome was arrested. Yet despite this anti-papist feeling and his outrageous double dealings with the French, Charles II survived for 25 years as King without provoking an outright confrontation with the Protestant majority of landowners and leading men of the state. He was clever, accommodating when necessary and probably too fond of his pleasures to act in a way that would really jeopardize his position. He never actually declared himself a Catholic until on his deathbed – ultimately he was not prepared to stake his crown for his faith.

A cultural revival

With the return of Charles and his court a new and rich period of cultural life began in London. Freed from the restrictions of Puritanism, composers and musicians, artists, writers, actors and dramatists now found a reward for their creativity. Once again

Medway. Peace negotiations were started straight away and a treaty was signed at Breda the same year. To many people in England and in Holland the greater menace came from the growing power of Catholic France under the absolute monarchy of Louis XIV, the Sun King. Charles aspired to the sovereign power of his cousin Louis and would have liked to have seen Catholicism triumphant in England. In 1670 he concluded the secret Treaty of Dover in which he pledged himself to bring the Catholic faith back to England and committed his country to an alliance with the French against the Dutch. This resulted in the Third Anglo-Dutch War

A view from One Tree Hill in Greenwich Park overlooking the Royal Hospital, now the Royal Naval College (below), designed by Sir Christopher Wren. To the extreme left is the Greenwich Observatory, founded by Charles as part of a move to revive an interest in science as well as in the arts.

portraits were commissioned from painters like Peter Lely as the rich and the powerful flaunted their proud bearing and gorgeous costumes to contemporaries and for posterity.

The most distinctive feature of Restoration London was the revival of the theatre. In July 1660, only two months after his arrival, Charles granted royal warrants to Sir William Davenant and Thomas Killigrew conferring on them exclusive and hereditary rights to raise companies of actors to perform in London. Since 1642, when professional performances had been banned by the Puritans, theatre had taken place clandestinely, frequently interrupted by soldiers and arrests. Now it was legal again but not widely so. Through their personal influence with the King, Killigrew and Davenant secured monopolies that were to fix theatrical activity in London for a century and a half.

Two theatres were thus founded: Killigrew's Theatre Royal – the King's Company – and Davenant's Duke of York Theatre, named after the King's brother. At first they were both housed in hastily converted indoor tennis courts but later moved to newly built premises with properly designed stages and greater seating capacities. Their repertoires included the Tudor and Stuart classics, sometimes adapted for modern audiences, and the work of new writers such as Dryden and Etherege. Special effects and elaborate scenery were an important part of Restoration drama and the stages were equipped with trap-doors, flying machinery and other devices. In 1669, for a production of Dryden's 'Tyrannic Love', the King's Company commissioned a scene of Elysium from the painter Isaac Fuller. It took six weeks to complete and eventually cost the fantastic sum of £335.10s. But the play was a great success, running for 14 days, taking £100 a day.

Many plays were performed only two or three times, and this rapid turnover meant that the actors were expected to learn at least ten parts a season and up to three a week. Working under these pressures they would rely on a small number of conventions in speech and gesture rather than develop the detailed characterization of modern actors. The opening nights were sometimes disasters because the actors 'had not their parts perfect'. Occasionally they would dissolve into attacks of giggles or ad-lib outrageously, but in the main they were professionals, skilled in their art. A common practice was for an actor or actress to become established as a certain character and always play that sort of part. Samuel Stanford, for example, was an actor who always played villains and was expected by his public to do so. On one occasion he was cast as an honest statesman but the audience refused to accept him in this role. They sat through four acts of the play expecting the apparent honesty to prove to be a disguise for the villany of his character and when they finally discovered that Stanford played an honest man to the end of the play 'they fairly damned it, as if the author had imposed upon them the most frontless or incredible absurdity.'

An important feature of Restoration theatre was the clause of the King's licence which for the first time permitted actresses to appear on the public

Charles was a keen theatre-goer and actively encouraged the revival of this art-form. During his reign theatres, such as the Duke of York's (above), became very popular. For the first time in years, actors and playwrights came out of hiding.

Simple pleasures and customs that had been banned under Cromwell were also revived – such as the Frost Fair (right) held on the frozen River Thames.

From 'bawdy house' to king's bedchamber. Despite her humble origins, Nell Gwynne's relationship with Charles II survived the test of time – and a series of more well-to-do mistresses. Her natural sensuality is captured on canvas (left) by one of Charles' favourite painters, Sir Peter Lely. With Nell is her son by Charles, later to become the Duke of St Albans.

A colourful picture of Restoration London – from court life to tippling in taverns – has been handed down via the famous diary of Samuel Pepys (right).

The National Portrait Gallery, London

stage. This opened the way for young women of low birth to find fame and fortune, at least while their good looks lasted. But despite the 'liberated' reputations of the Restoration, actresses received very little respect as women. Their profession was viewed as only marginally removed from prostitution.

'Pretty, witty Nell'

Nell Gwynne – the best known of Restoration women – was by her own admission brought up in a 'Bawdy House', a 17th century term for a brothel. She became an orange seller at Killigrew's Theatre Royal in Drury Lane and then the mistress of Charles Hart, one of the leading actors. She appeared in her first acting role when she was 15 and soon attracted devoted admirers for her talents as a comedienne, her quick tongue off-stage, and most of all for her beauty. The famous diarist Samuel Pepys was very taken with her and continually refers to her charm: 'Nelly, a mighty pretty woman', 'pretty, witty Nell', and 'and a mighty pretty soul she is'. He was delighted on one occasion when she kissed him in greeting. After Charles Hart her next great affair was with Charles Sackville, Lord Buckhurst, and so when she attracted the attention of the King, and became his favourite, she called him her 'Charles the Third'.

A contemporary wrote of Nell Gwynne that she was 'the indiscreetest and wildest creature that ever was in a court, yet continued to the end of the King's life in great favour . . . and was such a diversion to the King, that even a new mistress could not drive her away.' Yet even an actress who rose to these dizzy heights failed to achieve real respectability as a lady. Charles was reputed to treat her never 'with the decencies of a mistress, but rather with the lewdness of a prostitute, as she had been indeed to a great many'.

Royal sons, even those born on the 'wrong side of the blanket', were a different matter. Nell gave Charles two sons. The younger died in childhood but the first born, Charles Beauclerk, was created Baron Heddington, Earl of Burford and later Duke of St Albans. The story goes that during a visit of Charles to her house, Nell called her son to greet his father saying 'come here you little bastard'. When the King admonished her for using such a name she replied that His Grace had given her no other name by which

Although many considered the union beneath the King's brother, James, Duke of York, married his pregnant mistress Anne Hyde. James was far from being a faithful husband, but the marriage was relatively successful and provided England with two future queens.

to call the boy. So the King made him an Earl at the age of six and a Duke ten years later. Charles' dying wish is said to have been: 'Let not poor Nelly starve.' But although she was well provided for, Nell Gwynne only survived her royal lover by two years, dying in 1687 aged 37.

Pleasure palace

The remorseless pursuit of the pleasures of the flesh which so dominated court life was perhaps a reaction to the strict Puritanical morality. But it may also have been a response to a new age of money values in which hard cash and property contracts played a greater part in aristocratic marriage than romance and love. As Milton wrote in his famous work 'Paradise Lost': 'the law of marriage . . . is almost the groundwork of the law of property.'

Charles II's sexual appetites were legendary, but they were equalled and even excelled by his brother James. A court gossip, the French Comte de Gramont, relates one incident which particularly illustrates the atmosphere of court life. It also shows how accurately some of the scenes of Restoration Drama reflect the behaviour of the aristocracy. Charles II was moved to hear that his then favourite mistress, Frances Stewart, who had lately been refusing him on the ground of illness, was receiving the Duke of Richmond in her bedchamber. Bursting in after midnight the king found Frances Stewart 'a-bed, but not asleep, and he found then to boot, the Duke of Richmond sitting near her Pillow, who, in all probability was still less inclin'd to sleep than she.' Much embarrassed, the Duke exited over the balcony leaving the unrepentant Frances who protested to Charles that 'if she were not allowed to receive Visits from a Person of the Duke of Richmond's Quality, who came with Honourable Intentions, she were a Slave in a free Country'. The King stalked off vowed never to see her again and 'pass'd the most restless and uneasie Night he had since the Restoration.' In time Frances Stewart became the Duchess of Richmond.

James, Duke of York, had an even greater reputation for licentiousness, specializing in mistresses considered by his contemporaries to be

remarkably ugly – the King would quip that they had been given to him by the priests as penances! While in exile in Holland, James became infatuated with a lady-in-waiting, Anne Hyde, who was clever enough to secure from him a document agreeing to their marriage. After the Restoration, and pregnant with his child, she held him to the contract and he felt honour-bound to oblige although the King and his friends considered the match to be beneath him. The marriage produced two daughters, Mary and Anne, who were both later Queens of England. The responsibilities of marriage and parenthood, the death of Anne Hyde, and a second marriage to Mary Modena, an Italian, all took place without having any effect on James's voracious sexual appetites.

The court was thus, in Gramont's words: 'inspir'd by the Inclinations of a tender, amorous and indulgent Prince.' He describes how the nobility and the courtiers strove hard to improve their 'Talents as best they could. Some . . . by Dancing, others by Shew and Magnificence; some by their Wit, many by their Amours, but very few by their Constancy.'

The sexual mores of the court certainly dominated the values and the morality of the well to do in London, but did not meet with universal approval. Pepys was not averse to dalliance – he used to fantasize in church about his most recent sexual encounters and sometimes would visit two of his mistresses in one day. Pepys was employed in a high position at the Naval Office and he often got involved with women who were keen to secure promotion of their husbands. But Pepys, nevertheless, expected

During the early part of Charles' reign, England and Holland were frequently at war. However, the Dutch were a force to be reckoned with – they were not only a superior force, but also far more daring. The Dutch fleet sailed right up the Medway (left) and set fire to the anchored British ships. This victory brought the war to an end – although it was not to be the last.

William and Mary are shown on this delftware plate, produced around 1690. Two years earlier they had been proclaimed joint rulers of England.

more from his monarch and was especially displeased to hear that the king had treated one of his mistresses unkindly, 'which is very mean methinks in a prince, and I am sorry for it – and can hope for no good in the State from having a prince so devoted to his pleasure.'

Pepys' London

The diaries of Samuel Pepys and John Evelyn provide an invaluable source of information about everyday life during the Restoration. While Evelyn, an aristocrat, was more concerned to record the events of court and the King's Privy Council, Pepys was well placed to give a far wider panorama of Restoration London. His very successful career as one of the new breed of civil servants at the Naval Office gave him access to the peripheries of court life, ministers and leading men of the state but he himself was a commoner (the son of a tailor and wash-maid), and was familiar with the diverse pastimes, luxurious and commonplace, that the capital had to offer. He enjoyed musical entertainments, visits to the theatre and frequent meetings with friends in the many eating and drinking places of the city.

The sale of alcohol was only limited by law during the hours of church services on Sunday. Drinking establishments varied from the large and extremely respectable inns, to the small and sometimes squalid ale-houses. The tavern grew in importance during the Restoration. Specializing in the sale of wine they were usually large premises with a number of small and comfortable rooms suitable for private meetings, intimacy with a lady friend or solitary relaxation.

Most drinking places sold food also and eating out, especially at midday, was common practice. Meals varied from the extortionate price of 8s 6d at the French eating house the Chatelin in Covent Garden, to a more modest 1s to 2s 6d for dinner at a tavern, while snacks, such as pies, sea-food and cold meat, could be had for a few pence.

The coffee house, too, gained immense popularity. First introduced in Oxford in the 1650s, the idea soon caught on in London. Because of the reintroduction of censorship – all but official newspapers and publications were banned – these houses became centres, not only for gossip and for business transactions, but also for the spreading of news, political discussions, and places where groups of dissenters congregated – for this reason they were often threatened with closure.

As well as sampling the entertainments of London, Pepys also witnessed at first hand two events that shook Restoration London – the Great Plague of 1665 and a year later the Fire of London. The fire left much of London burnt out and derelict and the re-building in stone, to replace the cramped and largely wooden Medieval structures, took several decades to complete. The new St. Paul's cathedral, designed by Christopher Wren, was opened in 1697.

Undoubtedly, the libertine spirit of the Restoration was most keenly felt in London, where the well to do were celebrating a rebirth of the arts and enjoying an extravagant social life. But the new freedom to enjoy oneself was felt far and wide. Elsewhere in England old customs, such as dancing

In the aftermath of Charles' reign England became less 'merry'. Hundreds of Protestants were sentenced to death or to transportation by Judge Jeffries (right) after they rebelled at the Catholic James' succession to the throne.
After being proclaimed king, William went on to defeat his father-in-law and predecessor at the Battle of the Boyne in 1690 (above). This was the second time since his escape to France in 1688, that James' attempt to reclaim his crown had been thwarted. In 1689 the Declaration of Rights was drawn up by parliament, clearly defining its role and ensuring that no Catholic could succeed to the throne.

commandment at every opportunity!

So well known were his religious intentions that his succession on Charles' death in 1685 prompted a Protestant rebellion in the West country led by the Duke of Monmouth, the illegitimate son of Charles I. This was speedily suppressed, Monmouth was executed and at his Bloody Assizes the Hanging Judge Jeffries sentenced 300 rebels to be hung drawn and quartered and a further 1000 to transportation to the West Indies. Thus strengthened, James proceeded to suspend the laws that excluded Catholics from positions of power, culminating in 1688 in an order that his 'Edict of Tolerance' should be read out in all churches across the land. In the same year his second wife, Mary Modena, produced a son. Rumours were rife that the baby had been smuggled into the royal bedchamber – so strong were the Protestant fears of a Catholic line of succession.

William and Mary

In Holland, William decided that he could afford to wait no longer, and with a formal invitation signed by seven leading Protestant noblemen and clergy he invaded England in November 1688 with an army 12,000 strong. William was a skilled military strategist, James was not. As James vacillated in London his supporters melted away and with them his confidence. By the end of the year he had fled to France. So parliament was able to give the revolution a constitutional appearance – James was said to have abdicated – and by a combination of right, might and fait accompli William and Mary were crowned joint rulers. In 1690 William defeated an Irish and French army led by the ill-fated James at the Battle of the Boyne and then went on ruthlessly to subjugate Ireland as Cromwell had done 50 years before.

William, for Mary ruled in name only, was a new style of monarch – an experienced ruler and a professional soldier. Unlike his Stuart predecessors, he understood the working of money and the rule of property. He wasted no time in placing the accounts of the royal household under his meticulous scrutiny and generally became far more involved in the business of government than James or Charles had been. William had autocratic methods but he exercised his power through parliament instead of trying to circumvent it. The religious question which had so dominated politics during the Restoration was no longer an issue which divided king and parliament. The papist threat had been finally dealt with in England and the Protestant star was now well in ascendant.

Certain aspects of court life did, however, remain unchanged. The same nobility patronized the same artists and musicians. Purcell, for example, had been appointed as composer to the King in 1677 and he went on working as before, writing the music for Mary's funeral in 1694, the year before his own death. But the general demeanour of court had changed. Gone was the licentious romping of the 'Merry Monarch' and in its place a more sober and pious atmosphere in which drinking, swearing and immorality were actively discouraged, while regular worship and frugality were set by the monarchs as examples to be followed. Had an astrologer offered his services to William and Mary, as one did to Charles II, he would doubtless have been directed to a religious text – not, as with Charles, taken to Newmarket with the royal party and requested to pick out winners for the King to bet on!

around the Maypole and the Frost Fairs, were reintroduced, and for the first time children were able to play sports and games.

'Dismal Jimmy'

Charles' brother James was a rather different character – less subtle politically and more of a fanatic about Catholicism. He converted to the faith in the late 1660s in secret and became gloomily preoccupied with his papal 'mission' – Nell Gwynne used to call him 'dismal Jimmy'. Needless to say James' religious convictions did not put an end to his philandering and he continued to break the seventh

THE GREAT COMPOSERS

Antonio Vivaldi

1678–1741

As well as being a composer, Antonio Vivaldi was one of the greatest ever violin virtuosos. As a contemporary wrote, Vivaldi's playing 'quite confounded me, for such playing has not been heard before and can never be equalled'. Like many Baroque composers, Vivaldi was extremely prolific: he composed at least 450 concertos, as well as sonatas, operas and cantatas. He is, however, most celebrated for his programme music (that is, a piece of music that describes an idea or image). Of his programme music, the Four Seasons violin concertos are perhaps the best known. Vivaldi's fame, both as a composer and virtuoso, waned after his death until the 19th century, when the revival of interest in Johann Sebastian Bach – whose Brandenburg Concertos show Vivaldi's influence – led to the rediscovery of his music. Today Vivaldi is seen as one of the greatest, and most popular, of Baroque composers.

Antonio Vivaldi – called the 'Red Priest' because he had red hair and was in holy orders – was employed for many years by the Ospedale della Pieta in Venice, and there he wrote some of his finest music. The following pages describe that institution, as well as Vivaldi's later life as a wandering virtuoso. Vivaldi's music is, like Baroque music in general, extremely popular, but his Four Seasons violin concertos are almost certainly the best-known and best-loved of all his works. The Listener's Guide *analyzes the concertos in detail, showing how accurately the music depicts the accompanying sonnets to present an unrivalled evocation of the seasons. Vivaldi travelled a great deal, but he always returned to his native city of Venice. As In the Background describes, Venice was past her greatest days, but she was still a centre of European culture and formed a fitting backdrop to Vivaldi's music.*

COMPOSER'S LIFE

'The red priest'

Though ordained as a priest Vivaldi's passion was for music as much as religion, and the fervour which might have had a more pastoral outlet is in his music – the triumph of Baroque style.

The pen and ink sketch of Antonio Vivaldi (above), by Pier Leone Ghezzi, is the only known authenticated portrait of Vivaldi.

Vivaldi's father, Giovanni Battista Vivaldi, was a violinist in the orchestra of St Mark's, Venice (right). Vivaldi himself played violin here when he occasionally stood in for his father. It was in churches like St Mark's that a blend of religious and musical elements became firmly established and for which 18th-century Venice was noted.

A view of the San Martino parish of Venice (right) where Vivaldi was born. He spent much of his life here and this view is probably very similar to what he would have seen.

Canaletto 'S. Giuseppe di Castello'. Private Collection, Milan/Scala

P. Longhi 'Sacred Ordination'. Querini Stampalia, Venice/Scala

Given Vivaldi's humble origins it was not surprising that he should be directed towards a career in the church. It was a career which offered advantages in terms of social mobility to those who were otherwise excluded by birth. He received the tonsure from the Patriarch of Venice on 18 September 1693 and just over nine years later, in March 1703, was ordained as a priest in a ceremony similar to that shown left.

On the day Antonio Vivaldi was born in Venice an earthquake shook the city. He was given an emergency baptism, but it is not known for certain if this was because of the earthquake or because he was not expected to survive the frail and sickly condition with which he was born – thought to have been either asthma or angina pectoris.

In his lifetime Vivaldi made an international reputation yet for almost three centuries following his death his work sank into obscurity. Today, the 'red priest' (a nickname he acquired because of his red hair) has finally achieved the acclaim due to him and is recognized more than any other composer of the early Baroque period to have laid the foundations for the mature Baroque style compositions.

The red hair may well have been inherited from his father, Giovanni Battista, a baker's son who was engaged as a violinist at St Mark's Cathedral on 23 April 1665 under the name Rossi – literally, red-head! It is thought that Vivaldi's father may also have been a composer – an opera entitled *La fedelta sfortunata* is now attributed to him.

Despite the fact that he was sickly, Antonio, the eldest of six children, was destined from early child-hood to go into the priesthood. From 18 September 1693 to 23 March 1703 (the period between his tonsure and ordination), Antonio trained for the

Correr, Venice/Scala

Carlo Goldoni (above) was a talented young Italian dramatist who wrote libretti for one or two of Vivaldi's operas. From 1733 to 1735 Vivaldi wrote several operas for San Angelo and the Grimani theatre of San Samuele to which Goldoni was attached. They collaborated on Griselda *and* Aristide.

priesthood with the Fathers of San Geminiano and of San Giovanni in Oleo. Apparently, as a result of his condition – *Strettezza di petto* (tightness in the chest) – he received permission to remain at home with his parents in the district of San Martino.

As a youngster Antonio was taught the violin by his father and occasionally during his training for the priesthood stood for him as violinist in the orchestra of St Mark's Cathedral.

In Venetian society there was nothing wrong or even eccentric for a priest to be engaged in musical activity. Vivaldi's case was special, though, because of his illness and soon after his ordination in 1703 he gave up saying Mass and became a simple abbé with no pastoral duties. Some commentators on his life have suggested that full-scale pastoral activities might have got in the way of his music and that his decision not to say Mass was based on self-interest!

However, whatever the reasons for his withdrawal from pastoral duties he was outwardly a very religious man. Carlo Goldoni, the famous Venetian poet and playwright in his memoirs recalled a meeting with Vivaldi:

'I went to Abbé Vivaldi's house and found him surrounded by music and with his breviary in his hand. He rose, made the complete sign of the Cross,
put down his breviary, and made me the usual compliments. After a short opening conversation the Abbé took up his breviary once more, made another sign of the Cross, and did not answer.

'Signor', I said, 'I don't wish to disturb you in your religious pursuits; I shall come another time.' Vivaldi continued the conversation, however, walking about with his breviary, reciting his psalms and hymns . . . .'

Violin master at the Pietà

In September 1703, Vivaldi was engaged as *maestro di violine* at an extraordinary Venetian institution, the Conservatory of the *Ospedale della Pietà*. This 'hospital', affectionately referred to by its Italian diminutive, *ospedaletto*, was rather like the London Foundling Hospital of Handelian fame. There were four such hospitals in Venice. They were all charitable institutions orginally founded to receive orphaned, illegitimate and abandoned girls. The girls were given an education at the city's expense and, in the main, lived a closed life, some taking vows as nuns and living a convent-like life within the hospital walls. The girls were divided into two categories: those who received a general education and those who were given a specifically musical education.

The *figlie di coro* (girls of the choir) received

excellent training in singing and instrumental techniques. Many of them were extremely talented and the governors employed the best possible staff as teachers of music. Given the lack of information surrounding the parentage of some of the girls, some were simply known by their forenames and the instrument on which they were most proficient. There were great profits to be made from the musical activities of the 'hospitals' and the governors used these finances for the welfare of the institutions themselves.

Concerts were held every Sunday and feast-day and the level of general music-making that went on made it seem as if there was a concert every day. A British traveller, Edward Wright, visiting Venice in the early 1720's, when Vivaldi's fame was at its height, wrote favourably of the girls of the hospitals:

'Those who would choose for a wife one that has not been acquainted with the world go to these places to look for them, and they generally take all the care they can they shall be as little acquainted with the world afterwards . . . Every Sunday and holiday there is a performance of music in the chapels of these hospitals, vocal and instrumental, performed by the young women of the place, who are set in a gallery above and, though not professed, are hid from any distinct view of those below by a lattice of ironwork. The organ parts, as well as those of other instruments, are all performed by the young women. They have a eunuch for their master (sic) and he composes most of their music. Their performance is surprisingly good . . . and this is all the more amusing since their persons are concealed from view.'

Not all the girls or nuns in the hospitals, though, could have claimed to make such a favourable impression. Not all the girls took their vows to be nuns and, consequently, lived quite different lives. Another commentator gives quite a different picture to the other:

'. . . even after having taken their vows they maintained worldly practices and dressed elegantly . . . their bosoms only half covered by narrow pleated bodices of silk . . . The stillness of the cloister was sometimes broken . . . by the merry

Francesco Guardi: 'Venetian Gala Concert'. Alte Pinakothek, Munich. Joachim Blauel/Artothek

shouts of the young aristocrats as they danced with the nuns, who would go so far as to stay out all night with their lovers.'

First composition published

For his Pietà pupils Vivaldi wrote some of his finest music, and experimented with form and instrumentation.

Two years after his ordination Vivaldi published his first music, a set of 12 Trio-sonatas. The work was dedicated to a Venetian nobleman Count Annibale Gambara and was printed by Sala, a well-known Venetian publisher.

Vivaldi's second work, a set of violin sonatas, was dedicated to an illustrious royal visitor to Venice, King Frederick IV of Denmark. King Frederick arrived in Venice on 29 December 1708, and the next day attended a concert under Vivaldi's direction at the Pietà. By 1709, the actual date of publication of his opus 2, Vivaldi was working on the composition of the concertos for various instruments for which he soon became famous throughout Europe. He composed violin concertos, which he played himself, and

One of the more illustrious visitors to Venice during the Carnival season of 1708 was Frederick IV of Denmark (right). The day after his arrival in Venice he attended a concert under Vivaldi's direction at the Pietà. Vivaldi dedicated his Opus 2, a work consisting of 12 violin sonatas to the King.

Archiv für Kunst und Geschichte

Concerts in Venice (left) were very lavish and were attended by people who had travelled far and wide to listen to the many excellent vocal and instrumental performances. It is a mark of the excellence and musical standing of the young ladies of the 'hospitals' that they performed for audiences of the highest calibre. In the scene, left, the combined musical forces of the 'hospitals' can be seen playing at this state occasion. Vivaldi was violin master at one of these 'hospitals' – The Pietà – and wrote much of his best music for the pupils there.

A particularly Venetian institution, the convent parlour (below) was a social setting where games were played and music performed. Not all of the young ladies in the 'hospitals' were there of their own free will, some having been admitted by their parents to prevent unsuitable marriages. It was for their pleasure and entertainment that the convent parlour became such a jolly place.

concertos for other instruments to be played by the young ladies of the Pietà. These concertos were performed not only in the hospital galleries but also in churches, where they sometimes replaced the standard service music and the dazzling virtuoso violin playing by the maestro during church services was all part and parcel of the performances.

Vivaldi's position at the Pietà was renewed annually by the governors but in February 1709 they voted to discontinue his appointment. It is likely that the post was temporarily abandoned rather than that Vivaldi was guilty of any misconduct as two years later in September 1711 he was re-elected to his former post. From then onwards, although he was re-appointed, opposition to his appointment mounted steadily. Again, in March 1716, he was not re-elected but surprisingly was given a position with higher responsibility instead – the Master of music (*maestro de concerti*).

The position became available because three years before, a previous Master, Gasparini, had obtained sick leave (from which he never returned) and his successor was not much of a composer. This gave Vivaldi the opportunity to compose sacred music for the Pietà. The governors were so pleased with his efforts that in June 1715 they gave him a special payment of 50 ducats for a mass, vespers, 30 motets and other works which he wrote for them. The oratorio was *Moyses Deus Pharaonis* of which only the libretto has survived. This was followed a year later in 1716 by *Juditha triumphans,* a brilliant work with spectacular writing for high trumpets. In recent years this has become one of Vivaldi's most popular religious pieces.

Fame outside Venice

Vivaldi's fame soon began to spread far beyond his native land. His first two works were published in Venice in the old-fashioned 'music type' which had been in use there for centuries. In 1711, like many other Italian composers, Vivaldi moved his publishing activities from local firms to an Amsterdam publisher Etienne Roger. This firm and its successor Le Cène, were publishers of engraved music, very different to the existing music printing in Italy and far easier to follow. This move made his music available to a wider audience and as a result contributed to his fame and popularity.

In his preface to their first collaboration Vivaldi mentioned Roger's new technique. *L'estro armonico* published in 1711, Vivaldi's opus 3, was the single most influential music edition of its time. Dedicated to Ferdinand, Grand Prince of Tuscany, it consisted of 12 concertos for various combinations of strings. The publication of this work not only marked the change in reproduction methods but it also reflected the growth in demand in northern Europe for the latest Italian music.

It was not long before Johann Sebastian Bach obtained a copy of this new set of concertos. He was so fascinated by them that he transcribed a large number of them for keyboard instruments. Ironically, it was the renewed interest in Bach in the 19th century which led to the first investigations into Vivaldi's work.

Vivaldi followed the publication of *L'estro armonico* with *La stravaganza,* in 1714 – a set of 12 violin concertos dedicated to Vettor Delfino, a member of the Venetian aristocracy and a former pupil. The next 3 publications (opp. 5, 6, 7) of the years 1716–17 were ordered from Vivaldi by Roger who

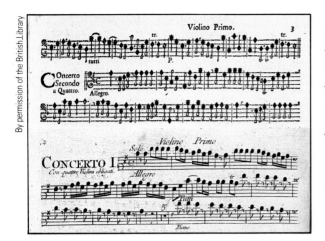

The local Venetian method of music printing from type (above) was difficult to read and laborious to produce. Vivaldi and other Italian composers changed to an Amsterdam firm of publishers, Roger. Roger's engraved copy (below) was elegant and readable and could be reproduced more easily.

had them engraved at his own expense – a rare practice indeed, and one which showed Vivaldi's great popularity.

Interest in the opera

From 1710 Vivaldi had followed his father's interest in opera. He began his operatic career in 1713 with a performance at the summer resort of Vicenza of a work entitled *Ottone in Villa.* His regular association was as a composer and impressario at the Teatro S. Angelo in Venice. For the opening of the 1714–15 season he composed his *Orlando finto pazzo.* He composed a pasticcio (a work consisting largely of borrowings from other compositions), *Nerone fatto Cesare,* and two operas before 1717. Then, for the San Moisé theatre, he wrote three operas between 1716 and 1718.

The travelling composer

The year 1718 marked the beginning of a long period of travel for Vivaldi, connected largely with operatic commissions in northern Italy. During this period the composer retained at least a nominal association with the Pietà in Venice, and whenever he returned, he took up at least part of his duties there. The first long stay was from 1718 to 1720 in Mantua, a city-state which was governed for the ruling Hapsburgs by Prince Philipp von Hessen-Darmstadt, a noted music lover. Vivaldi became *'maestro di cappella da camera',* a title he retained even after his departure. Rome was the next port of call and Vivaldi spent several carnival seasons (1723–4, possibly 1725, too) there. He played twice before the Pope and had his portrait brilliantly done in caricature form by Pier Leone Ghezzi. This portrait which still survives is the only authenticated likeness made during his lifetime. In Rome Vivaldi entered the charmed circle of Cardinal Pietro Ottoboni, formerly Corelli's patron and friend, and one of the first to recognize the talents of George Frideric Handel. Ottoboni, the Chancellor of the Vatican, himself a writer, composer and patron, at once recognized Vivaldi's genius.

Rome held romance, too, for Vivaldi. He became associated with a young contralto singer named Anna Giraud (or Girò, in the Italian spelling), possibly through their connection at the Pietà where she was his protégée – contemporary sources there refer to her as 'Annina della Pietà'. It is thought that her sister Paolina became Vivaldi's nurse. Both girls soon became regular and loyal members of the Vivaldi 'entourage'. The presence of two women in his household gave rise to comment, and it was believed that both women were involved in affairs

From 1718 onwards Vivaldi travelled a great deal. Rome (right) was one of his ports of call. It was thought that he spent at least three carnival seasons there and it is known that he was invited to play to the Pope twice. During one of his visits to Rome his Portrait was drawn by Ghezzi, and he came into contact with Cardinal Ottoboni, a celebrated music patron.

From 1710 Vivaldi continued to develop the interest in opera that he inherited from his father. The scene (left) from a period when Vivaldi was composing for the opera gives a clear picture of audience and singer participation.

with him. It was on account of these alleged relationships and his refusal to say Mass (on grounds of ill health, according to Vivaldi) that the clerical authorities later banned him from appearing in Ferrara, a papal domain.

From 1726 to 1728 Vivaldi was back in Venice concentrating on his activities as composer and impressario at the S. Angelo theatre.

His instrumental works continued to be published by Roger, and thus ensured the spread of his international reputation. *Il cimento dell'armonia e*

dell'inventione (the contest between Harmony and Invention) op. 8, appeared in 1725 and was dedicated to Count Wenzel von Morzin, a Bohemian nobleman. Vivaldi became a kind of long-distance *maestro in Italia* to Count Morzin. Opus 8 includes *The Four Seasons* which has become, since its spectacular resuscitation in 1939 at a historic concert in the Palazzo Chigi in Siena, one of the most popular pieces of 18th-century music. It was the first great instance of so-called programme music in Vivaldi's work and created a profound impression throughout Europe. It was in the repertory of Prince Esterhazy's orchestra at Eisenstadt before Haydn became its director in 1761. This work circulated in manuscript form before it was published by Le Cène. This was followed by the publication of opp. 10–12 before 1730, which are the last compositions considered to be by Vivaldi.

Vivaldi had dedicated his opus *La cetra* to the Austrian Emperor Charles VI, whom he met in 1728, possibly in the Adriatic seaport of Trieste. Charles thought highly of Vivaldi and may have played for him in Vienna in 1733.

Although his Amsterdam publishers were now issuing his music at their expense and paying him a generous fee, Vivaldi felt that he could do better by selling his works individually and in manuscript copies. He expressed dissatisfaction and voiced his intentions to a visiting British traveller, Edward Holdsworth.

Edward Holdsworth, an English classical scholar made many trips to Italy as tutor and companion to young gentlemen on the Grand Tour. In Venice he met Vivaldi, and in a letter (left) to Charles Jennens (Handel's friend and patron) he notes Vivaldi's terms for the sale of manuscripts.

Mauro Pucciarelli, Rome

In the years 1733–5 he was again the principal composer at S. Angelo in his home city of Venice, but his interests were still more and more directed towards the mainland, where he promoted opera in centres like Verona, Ancona and Ferrara. Because he was banned from Ferrara he could not personally supervise his operas there, so he had to rely on the help of local impressarios in whose scrupulousness he had little faith.

One of his more diverting foreign trips, was to Amsterdam to celebrate the centenary of the Schouwburg Theatre. There, on 7 January 1738, Vivaldi played violin concertos in the town which had witnessed his earlier publishing triumphs. In March 1738, Vivaldi's long asssociation with the Pietà was finally terminated, due to his long absences. Despite this, the association was to continue.

A final triumph in Venice

In 1739, Vivaldi was back in Venice producing operas, but his contemporaries record that his music was no longer so popular with Venetian audiences. Yet in December 1739, shortly before he left Venice for the last time, he was to have a final triumph there when Prince Friderick Christian, King of Poland and Elector of Saxony, visited Venice. There was an elaborate concert at the Pietà – all the surrounding canals were illuminated, and Vivaldi presented a series of new works. Luckily, the scores were taken back to Dresden and preserved by the king. Now known as the 'Dresden' concertos they form a valuable part of the Vivaldi archive.

The fact that Vivaldi's popularity had waned in his native land may have been one of the reasons that made him set off on his last journey to Austria. Anna Giraud was in Graz in 1739–40 and may have prepared the way for this visit. Vivaldi obviously hoped that Emperor Charles VI would remember him and that he might be offered commissions or an appointment. Before he left, after very complicated negotiations, the Pietà governors bought a large collection of his concertos and religious music.

Vivaldi left Venice in 1740 and set off for Vienna, but in October 1740 his great hope, Charles VI, died. Despite this setback to his hopes he continued on his journey. He probably thought it worthwhile to discover if there was any chance of preferment under the new régime. After all, the new empress's husband, Francis, had been the recipient of some of Vivaldi's dedications. Vivaldi arrived in Vienna in 1741. Nothing much is known of his life here except that he was old, forgotten and ill when he died on 28 July 1741. He died 'of internal flammation' in the house owned by the widow of a Viennese saddler named Waller. He was buried the same day in the Bürgerspital, a cemetary which no longer exists.

At the funeral six choirboys of St Stephen's Cathedral, including the young Joseph Haydn, sang the Requiem Mass. The event and the distressing circumstances of his poverty were recorded by a contemporary Venetian chronicler:

'The abbé Don Antonio Vivaldi, an excellent violinist called the 'Red Priest' and a highly-esteemed composer of concertos, in his time earned 50,000 ducats, but because of immoderate prodigality died a pauper in Vienna.'

In 1740, Vivaldi found that his work was not as popular with Venetian audiences as it had once been. This may have been behind his decision to travel to Vienna (top) where he hoped for new commissions or favours from the Emperor. It was, however, to be his last journey. He died in Vienna on 28 July 1741. The extract from the account books of St. Stephen's Cathedral (above) shows how little was spent on his funeral – that of a pauper.

LISTENER'S GUIDE
The Four Seasons

The violin concertos that make up* The Four Seasons *are masterpieces of 'programme' music, recreating in delightful detail the changing seasons in all their moods and colours.

Venice, the violin and Vivaldi . . . these three are inseparable, and nowhere more so than in *The Four Seasons*. These are violin concertos, and from the first vivid notes of *Spring* we feel, both delightfully and powerfully, the light-heartedness and Venetian self-confidence of Vivaldi at his best and most characteristic.

The Four Seasons are masterpieces of programme music. The title tells us at once the essence of what we need to know. All of us – and not only Vivaldi's peasants, shepherds and hunters – live to that deep, slow rhythm of earth and skies that the seasons mark, and we respond to this music that so wonderfully evokes their cycle. What could be more natural than this *Spring* in which the small birds sing amid rustling leaves, streams murmur and shepherds sleep or dance? Or the lazy Italian heat of *Summer* in which even the

cuckoo sounds half asleep until wild winds and thunder threaten the well-tended crops? Or the harvest-time singing, drinking and dancing of the hunters' season, *Autumn?* Or a *Winter* in which a master musician's tone-painting makes us tremble in the snow, struggle against the wind, slip on the ice and even fall through?

No wonder, then, that *The Four Seasons* quickly achieved popularity following on their publication in Amsterdam in about 1725 and then in Paris some four years later. Even King Louis XV – on 25 November 1730, according to the *Mercure de France* – once commanded an impromptu performance of *Spring* in which several nobles of his court took part.

That date is well documented. Unfortunately for the historian, other more central ones are unknown. We do not know exactly when *The Four Seasons* were

composed, nor the date or place of their first performances. What we do know is that they are the first four of a set of twelve violin concertos published as Vivaldi's op. 8 and collectively entitled *Il cimento dell'armonia e dell'inventione* ('The Contest between Harmony and Invention'). By this rather weighty title Vivaldi is saying that he here offers a blend of intelligence and fantasy.

If the title of Vivaldi's twelve violin concertos op. 8 is slightly cumbersome, maybe this was because the whole concerto set was dedicated to a Bohemian Count called Wenzel von Morzin (1676–1737) who had to be addressed in the imposing terms reserved for the nobility of the time.

The dedication to Count Morzin, 'from His Highness's most humble, devoted and obliged servant Antonio Vivaldi', mentions a period in which the composer was this noble's *maestro di musica* in Italy. This seems to have meant only that he provided

Vivaldi's Spring – a joyous celebration of the season filled with bird song and dance – opens briskly and brightly.

Vivaldi (right) reveals the humility that had to be shown by a musician to his patron in his dedication of The Four Seasons *(far right) to Count Wenzel von Morzin.*

The violin solo of the second movement of Spring *evokes the lines of the sonnet: 'The goatherd sleeps his faithful dog at his side' (below).*

Spring (Concerto no. 1 in E)

A The spring has come, and joyfully
B Is greeted by the birds with happy song,
C And the brooks, at the breath of zephyr
                winds,
  Flow, gently murmuring. Meanwhile . . .

D Appear, covering the skies with black robes,
  Lightning and thunder, like omens —
E Then when they are still again, the small
               birds
  Turn again to their song of enchantment.

F And thus, upon flowering gentle meadow,
  Among the pleasant murmur of foliage,
  The goatherd sleeps, his faithful dog at his
               side.

G To pastoral bagpipe with festive sound
  Dance nymphs and shepherds under a
            beloved sky
  Of spring, radiantly appearing.

First movement
The first of the *Spring* Concerto's three

music when the Count requested it — in other words Vivaldi did not hold a full-time post — and in fact the dedication ends with a request that the patronage should continue.

Programme notes

Each of the four concertos is preceded by a poem in the fourteen-line sonnet form depicting the moods and events of the concerto itself. More than this, single lines and short sections of each sonnet are labelled with letters of the alphabet (A to G in *Spring,* and as much as A to N in *Winter* with its riot of descriptive detail), and in turn the musical score itself is marked with these letters as well as the relevant lines of the poem. There are even one or two extra

bits of verbal information, e.g. 'Bird Song' at the solo violin's first entry in *Spring,* and 'Lassitude from the Heat' at the beginning of *Summer.*

It is not known who wrote the sonnets because they remain unsigned. Vivaldi knew plenty of authors who might have provided this literary material. Nevertheless there is some ground for thinking that Vivaldi himself composed them as a 'programme' for the music. If, as seems likely, the sonnets were written after the music itself, who better to tailor literary material to the existing music than Vivaldi? Whatever the truth, the poetry and the music appear as a complete and natural unity, as if conceived simultaneously. In the printed score each poem is labelled *Sonetto Dimostrativo* – 'Explanatory Sonnet'.

movements is in a brisk Allegro tempo: and the arrival of spring is merrily greeted by the orchestral strings and harpsichord, the lively pace and rhythm as well as the alternating loud and soft tone preventing any heaviness here. This section (marked A in the poem left) quickly gives way to the birdsong of B, evoked by the sweet trilling and chirruping of three solo violins, briefly answered by three bars more of the opening A music. Next it is the turn of the gentle breeze and murmuring streams (C). How simple, and yet how effortlessly right, is their music:

Example 1

Another brief return to the opening music, at a lower pitch than before, brings us to the miniature storm of the D section. This forms a contrast to the gentler preceding music, with its rapid (even jagged) upward scales and the thunder-rumble of *tremolando* strings, low in pitch. (*Tremolando* requires the players to draw the bow back and forth over the string very quickly to give a 'trembling' repeated-note effect.) Above all this the solo violin makes an agitated commentary. But it is not long before all is over – note the A music again, briefly, in a minor key – and once again the birds are singing (section E). A final return to the A music – technically the *ritornello* or 'recurrent idea' that marks out the shape of the movement – brings the Allegro to its end.

Second movement

The second movement, marked *Largo e pianissimo sempre* ('Spaciously and always very soft') evokes the F section, lines 9–11 of the *Spring* sonnet. Here Vivaldi presents us with a composite picture, carefully labelled with extra verbal indications in the score: the wonderfully relaxed solo violin melody that floats above is marked 'The Sleeping Goatherd' and the pairs of repeated notes played by violas in the bass are the 'barking dog' by his side. As for the violins' figure in the middle of the texture, these rustling leaves are a fairly close relative of the murmuring breeze and stream music of Example 1 in the first movement. This gentle picture gives way in turn to the 'Pastoral Dance' of the Allegro finale. Perhaps the sustained bass notes at the start and also elsewhere in this movement are intended to suggest the drone note of a rustic bagpipe; at any rate, the dance character is unmistakable throughout. The mood of this G music, corresponding to

With the opening bars of Summer *a heavy exhausting heat descends making 'Men and animals alike languish while the pine burns.'*

the last three lines of the accompanying sonnet, is instantly created and sustained without too much change, though there is one rather wistful moment near the end where the soloist, in 'minor' mood, is left virtually alone by the other dancers.

Summer (Concerto no. 2 in G minor)

A *In the harsh season of hot sun*
Men and animals alike languish while the
pine burns:

B *The cuckoo unlocks his voice, and in quick*
accord

C *Both dove and goldfinch sing also.*

D *A gentle breeze blows, but suddenly is*
challenged
To dispute by the near North wind;

E *The shepherd-boy weeps, overcome*
By fear of the storm and his own fate:

F *His tired limbs are denied of rest*
By fear of lightning and wild thunder –
And the furious onslaught like mosquitoes
and wasps!

G *Ah, all too justified are his fears:*
The skies thunder and lighten, and hail
Breaks down the corn and the proud crops.

First movement
The first line of the *Summer* concerto's sonnet reminds us that, at least for an Italian peasant, this was not an especially pleasant season of the year: the spring's invigorating warmth has given way to a

In the second movement of Summer the tempo quickens as 'the skies thunder and lighten, and hail/Breaks down the corn.'

heavy heat. The lassitude of the opening section of the first movement makes the composer's marking *Allegro non molto* a considerable understatement: there is nothing 'lively' (the literal meaning of allegro) about this weary music, marked A in the score. At least the cuckoo is alive and singing (B, at a faster pace), its famous two-note call sketched out in the busy semiquaver figures of the solo violin. But it is noteworthy that even here the music is in the minor key, as indeed is the concerto as a whole, despite individual 'major' passages to relieve the tension. At C, after a moment of referring back to the A music, the soloist becomes the gently pleading dove, and after that the higher-pitched goldfinch. It is a relief to feel the 'gentle breeze' blown by the orchestra at D – but how suddenly all this is swept away by the 'impetuous winds', as the score has it! No wonder that, after a brief further reference to the A music, we hear the herdboy's quiet sobs at E, evoked by the solo violin. The storm is by no means over and cruelly returns to close the movement.

Second movement
Indeed the Adagio slow movement of *Summer* brings no real respite. The 'tired limbs' of the first phrase (section F) are shaken further by the fear of the storm and its effects: note, here, the alternation between slow and fast tempo. And with the finale, section G, marked Presto (fast), we are once again at the mercy of the full harshness of the elements that drive the music forward to its close – a close that is surprisingly implacable in mood for such a melodious and tender artist as Vivaldi.

Peter Paul Rubens 'La Kermesse'. Louvre, Paris/Edimedia

Giorgione. Detail from 'The Tempest'. Accademia, Venice/Bulloz

Autumn (Concerto no. 3 in F)

A *The peasants celebrate, in dancing and*
singing,
Their joy in the good harvest

B *And with the liquor of Bacchus they're so*
overwhelmed

C *That their pleasures are to be rounded off*
with sleep.

D *Thus, one after another they cease to dance*
and sing:
The warm air is so agreeable . . .
And this Season induces so many
To enjoy sweet slumbers.

E *At first light, the hunters set off for a chase*
With their horns, their guns and their dogs:

F *The game takes flight, and they follow its*
trail;

G *Already scared and exhausted by the great*
noise
Of guns and dogs, wounded it tries

H *To flee from the danger, but dies at the end*
of its strength.

First movement
The *Autumn* concerto begins with a cheerful and distinctly tipsy dance, very different from the dance that ended *Spring*. The A music (which, as before, is to return at intervals during the movement)

here seems almost to mark out degrees of intoxication as the warm Italian wine flows abundantly in these harvest-time revels. At B, the solo violin is given a passage that Vivaldi actually labels 'The Drunkard' and which wanders uncertainly through the whole range of the instrument, for all the world like someone staggering about 'under the influence'. As Nikolaus Harnoncourt has written, 'his hiccups are imitated as is his thick, awkward speech, he falls down and then gets up again: soon there are several of them, who eventually fall asleep, their whistling breathing clearly discernible' (he probably means the quiet but somewhat 'hee-hawing' section marked C). The movement ends with the A music again, this time faster than at the start – Allegro molto instead of Allegro.

Second movement

Vivaldi's riot of description in this *Autumn* concerto continues with a slow movement entitled 'Sleeping Drunkards'. Here the strings are muted and the harpsichord plays restful arpeggios (broken chords, i.e. with the notes in sequence instead of together). This Adagio is a beautiful movement and slightly mysterious in mood: it even seems to end on a kind of

question mark since the final chord is not the usual tonic or key chord. This, of course, is the D section of the accompanying sonnet. So far we have carried through one episode, from dancing and singing to wine-induced sleep. But for the final movement of this *Autumn* concerto Vivaldi offers a complete change, with the bracing atmosphere of the first-light departure of the hunters. The opening music – a *ritornello* as in the first movement, which is to punctuate and unify the proceedings – is a hunting-horn call, brisk and peremptory. We hear the horns, then the solo violin, in alternation until a definite change of mood comes where the pursued game breaks cover at section F, best identified by the solo violin's agitated triplets, starting in the lowest register and rising in panic.

Example 2

This in turn is answered (G) by an orchestral 'great noise of guns and dogs'.

Autumn *opens with the intoxicated tempo of wine-soaked revelry as 'The peasants celebrate, in dancing and singing their joy in the good harvest.'*

More of the same, together with references to the *ritornello* hunting horns, leads to the final H section in which (as represented by a weary solo violin that seems to look skywards for the last time) the unfortunate quarry dies. The hunters' rejoicing, to a reprise of their opening music ends the concerto.

Winter (Concerto no. 4 in F minor)

A *Frozen and shivering in the glittering snow,*
B *In the rude howling of a horrid storm,*
C *One moves at a run, stamping one's feet the while*
D *One's teeth chatter in the extreme cold;*

E *By fireside spending quiet contented days While outside the rain soaks all in sight.*
F *One walks on ice, and with slow paces*
G *For fear of falling, trying to walk with caution;*

H *Or steps out boldly, slips and falls headlong,*
I *Trying the ice again and running quickly*

L *Until the ice breaks, leaving there a hole...*

M *One hears emerging from their gates of iron*
N *Sirocco, North wind: all the winds at war –*
But this is winter; and yet it still brings
pleasure.

First movement

The *Winter* concerto, for all its first-movement marking Allegro non molto, makes a tiptoeing, tentative start, with shivering little trills (the A section), and the solo violin's entry at B brings no comfort, but the bluster of a 'horrid storm'. These two ideas alternate until the 'running' C section begins, loud and purposeful.

A brief return to the A music leads into the chattering teeth of D, with rapid repeated notes for the soloist placed icily in a high-pitched register. Finally, the whole orchestra joins in the chattering music to provide a fierce ending to the movement.

Second movement

After all this, we are ready for a contrast – which Vivaldi superbly supplies in a Largo slow movement depicting the contentment of sitting by a warm fireplace as the rain beats down outside. The person sitting in comfort is doubtless suggested by the spacious and relaxed melody given to the

soloist (compare the tune given to 'The Sleeping Goatherd' in the middle movement of *Spring*):

Example 3

The rain beating down outside is represented in the music by the pizzicato accompaniment of the orchestral violins, marked to be played 'loudly'. This is one of

Vivaldi's most attractive and spontaneous movements, divided clearly into two nearly equal parts – eight bars and ten bars – which, although beautifully unified in style and melodic contour, nevertheless have no two identical bars of melody. The mood of this E section, the whole Largo, does not change, which is doubtless wise after the rapid changes of the first movement.

The finale of *Winter,* too, brings rapidly

With some truly inspired touches in the Winter *concerto Vivaldi conjures up snow-bound landscapes and snapping ice.*

Understanding music: the Italian influence

The change from the polyphony of the Renaissance to the baroque style was a gradual one. But if one had to pin down the very beginning of the new style which was to dominate music for a century and a half until around 1750, then one would turn to Italy around 1600.

The Italian baroque style began with the music of Caccini, and also made an apearance in the later music of Giovanni Gabrieli. In this, one melody reigned supreme, unfettered by polyphonic interplay, and was accompanied by a subservient bass line (the continuo) – marking the break with the old polyphonic style.

But the most enduring legacy of Italy to the baroque style was undoubtedly opera; for it was in the music of Italy's great early 17th-century master, Claudio Monteverdi, that the Italian contribution to the baroque style can be heard at its most influential. From the first primitive examples of Peri and Caccini to the wonderfully mature examples of Monteverdi for the Italian court – such as *Orfeo,* and for the new public theatres – *The Return of Ulysses* and *The Coronation of Poppea* – the early Italian operas mark more clearly than anything the spirit of the baroque which was exported all over Europe as opera took root and flourished.

Italy's next major contribution to the musical language of the baroque was the development of tonal language. The new form for the expression of this, both in orchestral and chamber music, was the 'sonata'. Here, the decisive figure is Arcangelo Corelli, whose sonatas for violin and concerti grossi for orchestra established the new language with such a triumphant clarity that they became models that were admired and imitated by many other composers, especially in England.

Italy also developed a strain of instrumental virtuosity that set it ahead of the rest of Europe. Violins renowned to this day were made in Cremona by the Guaneri, Stradivari and Amati families, and as the 17th century turned to the 18th, Italian violinists scaled new heights of skill: composers such as Locatelli and Geminiani, pupils of Corelli, invented such extraordinary tests of playing skill that only legendary virtuosos, like Tartini, could improve on them.

The excellence of musical instruments and instrumentalists found the most satisfying expression in the concertato style. This evolved from a single-instrument sonata with continuo, through doubling of the main instrument and

The music of the Italian composer Monteverdi (above) had a marked influence on the development of the baroque style.

the continuo as in Corelli's *Sonate a tre,* opp. 1–4, to the style of interplay between several soloists and a larger group of 'accompanists', or tutti. The concerto grosso developed out of this, and Vivaldi's prolific output of nearly four hundred played no small part in popularizing the form throughout Europe. Though the invention of the piano at the beginning of the 18th century was credited to the Florentine, Cristofori, Italy did not produce great pianists, possibly inhibited by the brilliant harpsichordist, Domenico Scarlatti.

During the 18th century, Italian musicians exported themselves and their art with great vigour. The central European courts and their musical establishments were replete with Italian players. The number and importance of Italian words and terms of expression in contemporary musical language is a direct result of their influence at this time. By the second half of the century, it was even said that Italy was becoming empty of musicians, so wide was the demand for them to travel around Europe demonstrating their skills.

Pergolesi's operas and those of his contemporaries, such as Piccinni, helped to move the Italian mode of expression towards the classical era. The Italian influence on the baroque did not end with the sonata and concerto grosso. Involving as they did both comic and relatively serious characters, operas such as Piccinni's, with their elaborate concerted act-finales, pointed the way for the brilliant development of opera that was to flower in Mozart's humane comedies.

Tiroler Landesmuseum Ferdinandeum, Innsbruck

changing musical imagery as Vivaldi presents the remaining eight lines of the accompanying sonnet, with seven labelled sections of 'programme' to be reflected in the music. 'Allegro' may be the tempo marking for this movement, but it is a cautious Allegro indeed as the solo violin, virtually unsupported, starts gingerly to walk on ice (F). By G the orchestra, no less timidly however, is with him, but at H all are heading for a fall which duly occurs in descending scales culminating in a bump. At I the soloist is off once again, only lightly accompanied: (by the way, Vivaldi omits to use the letters J and K). The soloist proceeds through a fairly tense crescendo and a few slide-like descents to the point (L) where the ice actually breaks, again in somewhat jagged descending figures followed by a pause of apparent shock.

Now, as we read the sonnet for *Winter,* we steel ourselves for yet another loud onslaught of the wild winds. But the composer has a surprise for us. It is the sirocco, the south wind, that blows first — and its warm breath reminds us of milder weather (M). But now this is swept aside by the 'warring winds' (N): furious blasts and chatterings from both the soloist and the orchestra bring the *Four Seasons* set to an exhilarating close.

Quiringh van Brekelenkam 'A Man and a Woman by a Fire' (detail) National Gallery, London

In the second movement of Winter, Vivaldi allows some respite from the biting cold. The opening is in a slow languorous tempo, lulling us into the cosy warmth of the section of the sonnet marked 'E': 'By fireside spending quiet contented days/While outside the rain soaks all in sight.'

Great interpreters

I Musici (the ensemble)

I Musici came into being when a group of 12 students from the Academy of Santa Cecilia in Rome gave their first public performance together. The group had often met for private rehearsal and pleasure previous to this, but their first recital in 1952 gave rise to a need for a name. Due to the immediate success of the group, it stayed together as a professional body and the originally adopted name stuck. Within a year of the initial concert, I Musici travelled extensively in Europe completing tours of Spain, Portugal, Italy and France, as well as making a highly acclaimed début at the Venice International Festival of Music.

In the next two years, tours of England, Belgium, Holland, Austria, Germany and Scandinavia, as well as Eastern bloc countries, were all successfully undertaken. After this their popularity was assured. This quick acceptance was due at least in part to their enthusiasm for, and dedication to, music from the Baroque period; especially from the Italian Baroque composers such as Albinoni, Torelli, Bononcini and Gabrieli. Of course their performing accuracy and their prodigious ensemble virtuosity were well received by their public as well. With the aid of records such as their prize-winning 1956 recording of Vivaldi's *Four Seasons* their fame soon spread across the Atlantic and they quickly completed successful tours of both North and South America, making a particularly favourable impression in the USA. Return tours to the US in the 1960s have cemented their popularity there.

It is with Vivaldi that the group's name is most often associated, both on records and in the concert hall. I Musici has done as much as any other performing group to bring that master's music to the attention of modern music-lovers. They have recorded *The Four Seasons* concertos four times, and have made extensive recordings of the mass of concertos which Vivaldi produced so prolifically in his lifetime. Many of these further recordings are among the finest of their type to be found anywhere in the world such as the complete flute concertos, recorded with Severino Gazzelloni.

In more recent years, the group have diversified their performing repertoire, moving into the 19th century with works such as Rossini's string sonatas and Mendelssohn's string symphonies. They have also performed the works of such modern-day composers as Bartók, Benjamin Britten and Frank Martin with great distinction. They have now successfully completed over 30 years as an active and popular performing unit.

FURTHER LISTENING

Vivaldi concertos and choral works

L'Estro Armonico, op. 3
Although the 12 concertos that make up op. 3 had been in circulation for years before their publication in 1711, it was this grouping of them which made Vivaldi's name in Europe. Vivaldi's usual brilliance with the violin dominates the faster movements, while the slow movements often have an intense lyricism which was unparalleled in its day. The eleventh concerto is an undisputed masterpiece and contains a flawlessly worked out fugue.

La Stravaganza, op. 4
This collection of 12 concertos demonstrates Vivaldi's determination to create something new in concerto form. Principally, his division of the string orchestra into four parts and his allocation of a solo part for a single violin in all 12 concertos was to have far-reaching consequences for later composers. The work itself is brilliant Vivaldi, more harmonically advanced than op. 3, and with difficult technical problems for the soloist to solve. As such, it is an aptly-named collection, containing sumptuous and often exquisite melodies.

Gloria in D, RV 589
Although Vivaldi was ordained as a priest in 1703, it was ten years before he was given the opportunity to write any sacred vocal music. The 12-movement Gloria is one of his few widely-known choral pieces, and in it he displays a true gift for writing music with the human voice in mind, displaying great sensitivity to the text he is setting. This Gloria is an ideal introduction to a major area of Vivaldi's achievement as a composer.

IN THE BACKGROUND

'Serene republic'

*In Vivaldi's day Venice was enjoying its final fling
as the centre of European culture – a uniquely
important position that stemmed from deep roots
in the history of the city and its people.*

Venice, (below) sprang up from clusters of houses on piles built on a lagoon. Its position at the head of the Adriatic Sea – the crossroads between the east and west – helped it develop a powerful trading empire.

Right across the Baroque and Classical era, Venice, though well past its heyday, played out the final act of a centuries-old role of devotion to the arts. Like a living magnet the city attracted artists of every type – painters, sculptors, writers and musicians – and, in turn, spawned many of its own, like the Bellini brothers, Tintoretto, Goldoni and Vivaldi.

In music, to perform and succeed in Venice signalled brilliance and acclaim – and the cream of aspiring and established musicians flocked to the city. Promoted by an eager and sophisticated citizenry, an almost magical artistic spirit therefore sprang up and spread outwards. And it was against this cultural background influence that many composers worked, both within Venice and across Europe.

Just how and why Venice developed to become such a major cultural centre is the story of Venice itself.

The foundation of an empire

Uniquely different from other settlements in Italy – a series of village clusters, houses built on piles, canals dug between heights of land – Venice's unusual position on a lagoon dates back to the Dark Ages, when Latins fled there at various times to seek refuge from the warring hordes from the north. Its location at the head of the Adriatic Sea made it a natural focus for trade between Europe and points further east.

Part of the spirit of Venice stems from this proximity to and long connection with the East – a connection which lasted six centuries, from 1100 to 1700, during which Venetians held sway over the Mediterranean. Venetian power and influence extended to Byzantium and the shores of the Levant, south of the Ionian Isles and northwards to the foothills of the Alps. In her art, architecture, music and to some extent in her social structure, the influences of these different worlds are apparent – the mingling of Gothic, Byzantine, even Persian or Turkish elements made Venice one of the most exotic and cosmopolitan cities in Europe.

Venice's rise began with the first of a long series of bargains. The Byzantine Emperor Alexius Comnenus (1081–1118) desperately needed Venetian ships to help ward off the threat of crusading Norman knights rampaging across his territory, and to keep the Adriatic Sea free. In return for their help, the Venetian sea traders were given extraordinary privileges – tax-free commerce in Constantinople and most of the other imperial ports in the Adriatic, the Mediterranean and Aegean Seas. On the other hand, the Byzantines quite understandably looked at Venice almost as an outpost of their empire, and their own merchants traded freely in Venice. But Venice remained totally independent, its people subject only to the Doge.

Commercial power

Venice capitalized on its unique advantages with the Byzantine Empire to spread further afield, leading European trade into Egypt and from there into the Black Sea. The trade was in luxury goods – spices, furs, gemstones and in more substantial but just as valuable objects such as good timber, metals and grain. This trade laid the foundations for Venice's enormous import-export business.

The city never became a great industrial centre for manufactured goods, but it established one of the biggest industrial complexes of the Middle Ages – the Arsenal. This included vast ship-building docks, sailmaker's yards, rope spinners, and later, gunpowder and ammunition factories. The site lay at the edge of the city surrounded by a two-mile long castle-like wall with fifteen huge towers, built over the Zemelle islets, and was described by the historian Andrieux as 'the most formidable armoury and the mightiest naval dockyard in the whole of Europe'.

The key factor in its power was that the Arsenal was publicly owned, not a private venture, and specialized in warships. The skill and speed of the workforce, too, was legendary. At its peak, for instance, the workers could build a completely equipped galley in less than an hour.

From its foundation the Venetian fleet was notedly belligerent, sweeping the Egyptians out of the sea in the 12th century, winning advantageous trade terms from the King of Jerusalem and continuing their incursions up to the edge of the then Hungarian Empire. But the Venetians were not interested in conquest for territory – only for the commercial gains to be won from domination. This added to the increasing prosperity of the city state, for there was little attempt to set up extensive and expensive colonies in far-flung places, which would always require a military presence and a great deal of investment to sustain them.

The City of St Mark

The Doge or Duke of Venice was a rather curious head of state. He was a leader elected for life – not a hereditary king – and held only symbolic power. He could be replaced at will if he misbehaved in any way, and in official ceremonies he was constantly reminded of his captive position: he was always followed by a man bearing a broad-bladed sword to remind him of the beheading of the Doge Marino Falieri in 1355 for leading an abortive coup d'etat.

The Doge was the spiritual leader of a city founded on the cult of St Mark. Tradition held that the remains of the saint were brought ashore by two Venetian sailors, who had stolen the sacred bones from Alexandria and the Moslems who ruled there in 829. To Venetians, these links with St Mark were as important as the links Rome had with St Peter.

Saint Mark's basilica, started in the 11th century and modelled on the Byzantine Church of the Holy Apostles in Constantinople, was completed in the 15th century. It was both a shrine to the saint, and the chapel of the palace of the Doge, whose official position was chief magistrate of the Venetians, and mystical standard-bearer of Saint Mark.

The two aspects of Venetian life, the special heritage and commercial interests, came together symbolically in the Venetian ducat, the first and most important coinage in Europe in the Middle Ages, better recognized throughout Europe than any other. On one side of the gold coin St Mark is shown offering his standard to the Doge who kneels at his feet, wearing the strange pointed cap that was his badge of office. And outside the ducal palace at the

Of the many Doges of Venice, Leonardo Loredan (right), elected in 1501, was one of the most eminent. This portrait was painted by another famous Venetian – the brilliant artist Giovanni Bellini.

Marco Polo (right) was one of Venice's most famous sons. As a traveller, trader and adventurer he epitomized the Venetian spirit.

Mauro Pucciarelli-Roma

head of the staircase in the courtyard of St Mark's stand the Roman gods, Neptune and Mercury, gods of the sea and of commerce respectively – symbols of Venice's real life alongside its spiritual one.

Within the city itself, the internal economic organization gave Venetian merchants the most advantageous situation for expansion – without draining the city coffers dry. Taxation in Venice was kept at a low level, in order to give the entrepreneurial men sufficient spare capital to expand their enterprises. But in addition, the Venetians invented a special system of trading finance, called the *colleganza*. Simply, it meant that a silent partner put up two-thirds of the money required for a merchant voyage, while the active partner (the merchant who did the dealing abroad) put up only one-third. At the end of the voyage the merchant was given thirty days to come up with the proceeds of the sale of the merchandise, and split it fifty-fifty with the

Giovanni Bellini 'Doge Loredano'. The National Gallery, London

Vittore Carpaccio. Detail from 'The Meeting of St. Ursula and St Etherius'. Accademia, Venice/Scala

sleeping partner. Sometimes the voyagers invested no capital – a backer put up all the money needed, but in this case, the merchant got only one-quarter of the proceeds, the balance going to the backer.

This system had a highly original effect on society in Venice. Almost the entire population dabbled in trade, in commerce and foreign ventures. Rich old ladies, distinguished noblemen, sharper-brained investors like the Jewish community of money-lenders, all operated through the colleganza system (which gave rise to the phrase 'when my ship comes in'). The system created an unusual cooperation and tolerance among a population made up of many creeds and races. And, in this respect, the Venetians were different from their business rivals, the Moslems and Levantine Jewish communities, who would never dream of entering into business arrangement outside their own creed or even families.

Venice was remarkable for its self-help style of trading and government too – which affected many aspects of city administration. In later times, it was often said that there were few unemployed or destitute persons in Venice. The independence of action which the city state encouraged meant that the various trade organizations, the guilds or *scuoli,* as they were called, looked after their own activity, whether it was ship-building, cloth-weaving, glass-blowing or whatever – and looked after their brethren when they were sick or old. Each scuolo maintained a school and a hospital – the government of the city did little at state level to provide education or health care, so it was entirely a beneficial system. One of the proudest of all the scuoli were the *arsenalotti,* the men from the ship-building yards, who often formed the ducal escort on important holidays.

A grand façade

It was during the 15th century that Venice reached the height of its power, with control of all the main trade routes into Europe from the East. During this time, too, the city was being constructed – a majestic display of architectural styles ranging from the oriental splendour of its Byzantine-style churches to the Roman-classical palazzos of the aristocracy, and the particular version of Baroque style for which Venice became famous. The blending of all these styles of architecture, marble columns combined with ornate gilt and coloured fresco works of baroque and rococo forms, all floating over the canals, with a silvery haze of light patterning the varied walls, made Venice a matchless sight. When neo-classical edifices were later added, with the rise of the Palladian style of architecture in the 16th century, Venice became truly magnificent. The main thoroughfare of the city was the Grand Canal, and on its sides all the important places, business buildings and warehouses were built.

Following the great expansion of the 16th century, land space on the lagoon became even more crowded, and noble families took to building villas on the land around the bay of Venice. Only then did they begin to conform more to the pattern of aristocratic life in

In her heyday Venice boasted the mightiest naval dockyard in Europe. The skill of the workforce was legendary and trading vessels like those shown, left, enabled Venetian traders to travel as far afield as Egypt and China in search of valuable merchandise.

other urban centres of Europe, retiring to their estates in the summer, and living as much off the rent from their lands as from their trading business in the city itself. But true Venetian nobility always remained metropolitan. There were few enough of them anyway – the old families were listed in 'The Book of Gold', a register of aristocrats, and numbered just over 200. And there was no system at all for the enlargement of this noble elite. Making money or buying land did not permit entry into their ranks. So Venice was always ruled from the top by a select band of people who had little of their own commercial or political ambitions to pursue – unlike their ancestors.

The two main institutions of government, besides the figurehead of the Doge, were the great Council set up in 1296, and the executive Board of Ten, made permanent in 1334. Only noblemen whose fathers had served before them on the Grand Council were eligible to join, so that a 'hereditary political caste' was created. They were more interested in maintaining the status quo, civilized and generous as it was, than in progress or power.

In the end, the very stability of the social structure, everyone in their place and happy about it, con-

The true splendour of Venetian architecture is summed up in this romanticized view of the Piazzetta (right) looking into St Mark's Square. To the right is the Doge's palace, one of the finest secular Gothic buildings in the world. It was far more than just a ducal palace as it also held the council chambers, the courts, torture chamber and prison. In the background is St Mark's Basilica, modelled on the Byzantian style and built originally as the chapel of the palace. Still impressive, but not quite so grand, is the view of the Rialto bridge and surrounding area of urban Venice below.

Albert Emil Kirchner 'Piazzetta and Piazza San Marco, Venice.' Schackgalerie, Munich. Joachim Blauel/Artothek

Vittore Carpaccio. Detail from 'Miracle of the Reliquary of the True Cross.' Accademia, Venice/Bulloz

tributed to its downfall. The nobility of Venice dwindled steadily over the centuries. Their attitudes were traditional, uninventive. They lived forever in Venice's golden past when she was *La Serenissima* – the queen of the Adriatic. And as powerful new forces grew in the burgeoning cities of the northern countries of Europe, there was no forward-looking force in government to stop the rot.

The tide begins to turn

Venice managed to recover well after the first incursion on her trading supremacy was made by the Portuguese after Vasco da Gama found a new way through to the Spice Islands of the East, in 1497–99. But later, the English and the Dutch moved in, between 1590 and 1610. The move over to smaller ships with sails, replacing the heavier cargo-carrying rowing galleys of the Venetian fleet put paid to her sea power. Where once she had been technically in the vanguard with her shipbuilding, now she fell behind. Barbary pirates preferred to raid the slower-moving Venetian merchant ships than attack the new 'round ships' of the British and the Dutch. These were operated by professional sailors anyway, formidable adversaries in comparison with the slave crews of the Venetian galleys.

But it was not only the fall off in trade that brought Venice to the second rank in world power. During the 16th century, other ambitious monarchies in

Europe set their sights on expansion. The French, the Hapsburgs, the Spanish, and the Papal force of Rome joined together in the League of Cambrai. The Venetians, with their long history of intrigue and diplomacy, held out by siding first with one force and then another. By playing off the Hapsburg Maximilian, in league with the Pope, against the French, and then changing sides and pitching the French against the Hapsburgs, the city managed to emerge after 1517 almost intact against the forces of the league. But the tide was turning.

At this time, religious forces were splitting Europe into two camps – Protestantism in the north and Roman Catholicism in the south. Rome was, therefore, more determined than ever to expand as far as it could and to strengthen its power by demanding more loyalty from those territories which owed it religious allegiance. As a result, it was in no mood to be tolerant towards its wayward daughter – Venice. Loyalty and obedience from Venice were essential to help consolidate Rome's political and religious base. Having lived by its own laws, permitting a high degree of independence to flourish within its walls, and having flaunted its long connections with the 'heathens' of the east, Rome finally commanded that Venice toe the line.

The Venetians were, in the main, very devout. The religious orders, particularly the Jesuits, fanned the fires of religious zeal among the populace. But Venice itself reacted against this intrusion on its independence. Instead of aligning with Rome's demands, Venice arrogantly signed an alliance with the Turks just when the Hapsburgs were launching a Holy war against the Ottoman Empire in the name of Catholicism. This was the final straw. The city was placed under a formal edict. At first it was ignored, but in the end the powerful threat of Rome won out. All political decisions of the Doge were then scrutinized by Rome, through offices of the Catholic emissaries at the court.

The major reason why Venice finally agreed to obey was a visitation of the Plague in 1630–31. The disease had hit the city before, notably in 1575, but whereas on that occasion the city responded by setting up special hygiene rules, and reforms in administration to help the poor and sick, this time the blight of disease was seen as a curse from God for denying the rules of Rome, spiritually and politically – their civic as well as religious independence had, in effect, collapsed under the weight of such a powerful opponent.

High life in Venice

But even in decline, the atmosphere of Venice held a magnetic attraction for all who came to visit – and almost everyone of note did. Musicians, for example, would flock to Venice. The Venetians were great connoisseurs of music, and the chance to play in one of their many fine theatres and opera houses was a privilege indeed.

When Montaingne came in the late 16th century he was astonished to see the crowded hubbub of everyday life in the narrow streets – noblemen, nuns, mistresses, gamblers, gondoliers, Jewish merchants, fortune-tellers, newsmongers all plied their trade in

Venice was a city of culture and her wealthy families were keen patrons of the arts. One of many theatres, the S. Samuele (left), saw the performances of works by many composers – including several by Vivaldi.

close proximity. All the little bridges and streets were lined with attractive shops and market stalls, like the Bridge of Sighs, offering a wealth of practical and luxurious goods.

Courtesan life reached a high level of sophistication in Venice's day. Noblemen married late – if at all, the statistics revealing an unusually low rate of matrimony, which contributed to the fall in numbers and therefore the power of the ruling class. Courtesans flourished, and were allowed a degree of public status quite unseen in any other city; they were honoured, cultivated and influential.

Even married women had their own form of licence. It became customary for a woman, who had been immured throughout her single life within the walls of her father's home, to acqure a *cavaliere servente* upon marriage – or possibly two, three or four. These men, of equally noble birth, were her chaperones to take her out and fawn attentively upon her – in effect, legitimized lovers. One woman's husband might equally well be another's cavaliere servente. It was a most attractive way to make arranged marriages work. Sometimes, however, there would be no actual sexual relationship between the lady and her cavaliere. The lady would extend her passions to her hairdresser, while her cavaliere would pass a few obligatory frantic moments with the upstairs maid.

City of festivals and fêtes

Nothing so epitomizes the Venetians' love of gaiety and fun as the carnivals held in the city. The season extended for nearly half the year – from the first Sunday in October until Christmas, and then from Epiphany until Lent, with a further two weeks at Ascensiontide. For these months, all the citizens of Venice could dress up in white-faced masks (bautta) and big black cloaks (tabarro) obliterating their real identity and allowing them to pass through the streets with total anonymity – free to do whatever took their fancy. Anyone in carnival dress could enter any of the cafes, any of the gambling houses or ridotti, and have their fantasies realized in unpredictable encounters. On one occasion someone even spotted the Pope's emissary in mask and cloak and asked his blessing – to the shock of the onlookers.

Costumes under the bautta and tabarro were as elaborate a disguise as could be arranged. Favourite styles were drawn from the characters of the great

In the views of the Piazzetta (above) and the Piazzo S. Marco (right) the Venetian painter, Canaletto, captures the atmosphere of his home city. The hustle and bustle went on alongside the refined elegance of the well-to-do out for a stroll.

The Venetians' love of splendid architecture was founded on the art and skill of the many stonemasons (below) that the city supported.

traditional Italian folk comedy, the *Commedia dell'Arte* – the black-robed Doctor Graziano, the sad-faced Arlecchino, or the beautiful young lovers. But other favourite fancy-dress outfits reflected the glorious past of the city: flashing-eyed Turks, feathered Indians, or black-shrouded pirates and priests. Even nuns from the convents escaped at carnival time and joined their lovers to frolic in the dark and narrow streets, or take a prolonged, breathless ride on a gondola. The scandal of the nuns, with their low-cut dresses, queening in their salons where they entertained mixed company separated

from the world by only a light iron grille, was notorious. But the truth was that half of the convents in Venice were respectable closed orders. The remainder, however, which gave rise to the gossip, housed the cast-off daughters of the nobility, whose families were too poverty stricken to supply a good dowry. Consequently, as they were not nuns by choice many tried to lead as active a social life as possible both inside and outside the convent.

Other festivities included the spectacular *Fêtes Venitiennes* – seemingly held for no other reason than for having yet another ball, a banquet, a procession through the streets and waterways, or a series of fire-lit tableaux floating on the Grand Canal. Since Venice maintained her status as a centre of diplomacy and intellectual exchange right to the end, every visit of an ambassador, prince or other dignitary would be marked by a fanfare, a firework display or some other public celebration. Perhaps the most picturesque and moving of the regular annual spectacles was the Fête of the Sensa, so called because it was held on Ascension Day. For this the Doge of Venice acted out the longstanding ritual of his marriage to the sea. A huge galleass, the Bucintoro, decorated with the finest carving and gilding, was towed out of the Arsenal. On top of the deck the duke's throne, placed under a canopy, was surrounded by figures and statues representing all the mythical links of Venice's past. The great ship would sail out, followed by all the noble families and the foreign embassies in their private gondolas, richly painted and decorated for the occasion. Then a stream of lesser vessels, all garlanded and

decorated, with all the scuoli or guildmen wearing their brightest uniforms. When the procession reached the lighthouse at the Lido, in the bay, the Doge threw his consecrated ring into the waves, and said the words 'We wed thee, oh sea, in sign of true and perpetual domination'. Bells would ring, trumpets sound out, and the crowds of Venice cheer with force. On returning to the city, the people gathered in the grand square of the Piazza, for the greatest fair of the Venetian year.

Festivals and fêtes took up six months of the Venetian year. So, for many folk (such as the tooth-puller above) it was business as usual, while others paraded the streets in carnival masks and attended sumptuous regattas (below).

End of an era

Venice finally bowed low to Napoleon. In 1797, after he had stormed across the Austrian Hapsburg territories in northern Italy, he descended on the fading city and demanded that the Doge, its ruler, accept abdication.

When Napoleon's forces arrived they burnt the Bucintoro to cinders, all the better to strip off the gilding that had been applied to the boards. Goethe had described the ship as the perfect image of what 'the Venetians had been and believed themselves to be', and the loss of its ornament seems a fitting summary of the decay of Europe's longest-enduring and happiest republic.

And when Napoleon suppressed the scuoli it was said: 'In the name of liberty, in 1798, the people lost their corporate security and with it . . . lost all they had. In these straits they turned to government charity and became for the first time in their history a proletariat . . .'

In purely political and constitutional terms, the Republic of Venice came to an end. It had lasted intact from 1310 to 1796. But in a sense, this defeat was an afterthought. Venice had been in glorious decline for about two hundred years before that. However, no Venetian ever accepted it. Sumptuous, sophisticated life was maintained as ever.

The story of Venice cannot, therefore, be measured by such simple yardsticks as lost battles, unfavourable treaties and domination by a foreign force – its spirit, albeit in a humbler way, continued to live on.

Paris Bordone 'The Giving of the Ring to the Doge'. Accademia, Venice./Scala

The most splendid and elaborate of all the Venetian ceremonies took place every year on Ascension Day and marked the symbolic marriage of Venice to the sea. The ceremony began when the Doge received the 'wedding' ring in his palace (left), and then led a floating procession on the magnificent gilded galley – the Bucintoro – to the Lido where he cast the ring into the sea.

THE GREAT COMPOSERS

George Frideric Handel

1685–1759

George Frideric Handel was born in Germany, but became in 1726 a naturalized British subject. He composed a huge number of both vocal and instrumental works, and when he died, Handel was a figure of national importance. He has retained his popularity in his adopted country: in many English churches a Christmas performance of the Messiah is traditional. The Water Music and the Music for the Royal Fireworks are also frequently performed, most notably in the case of the latter in 1981, when the wedding of the Prince of Wales was celebrated with a recreation of the original firework display. In other countries, Handel's work was neglected until comparatively recently. However, with the more frequent staging of his operas and, with the current interest in early music, a move to a more 'authentic' style of performance, Handel's greatness is recognized by a wider world listening public.

Composer's life

Unlike many other composers – Vivaldi, for example – Handel did not come from a musical family, and his father, an eminent barber-surgeon, was opposed to his son becoming a musician. Handel senior was only persuaded to allow the boy to study music by the Duke of Saxe-Weissenfels, and then only on condition that his son continued with a general education that would enable him to study for his intended career of the law. Perhaps his father felt that music was not a respectable profession; certainly the theatre, which was one of Handel's main interests, still had a slightly disreputable reputation and, as Handel was to discover, was a very easy way to lose money. Throughout his life Handel loved Italian opera, and accepted the conventions of opera seria: the use of male contraltos and sopranos, and stylized arias and recitatives. After years of neglect – partly due to lack of understanding of these conventions – Handel's operas are being revived and are now appreciated as spectacles of great dramatic power.

COMPOSER'S LIFE

'Mynheer Handel'

Handel's search for a free musical climate took him to England, a country he adopted as his home and where he exercised his talents on a vast range of vocal and instrumental works.

One of the greatest composers of the Baroque period, George Frideric Handel was born on 23 February, 1685, in Halle, Germany. His father, Georg, a highly respected barber-surgeon, was 63 when his second wife, Dorothea Taust, gave birth to their son.

The young Handel soon showed a keen interest in music though he was not encouraged by his father, probably because he thought that a career in law would offer more prospects and stability.

Not much is known about Handel's early years, but Handel later told his first biographer that his father would not let him have access to a musical instrument. So he smuggled a clavichord up into the loft of the house – a small, gentle-toned keyboard instrument – on which he could practise secretly. Nevertheless, his talents must have been impressive for at some time during his childhood he was taken to the ducal court of nearby Saxe-Weissenfels, where the duke heard him play and advised his father to have him properly taught. This task fell into the hands of F. W. Zachow, organist of the Halle Liebfrauenkirche, who tutored Handel during his time as a pupil at the local grammar school. From this respected and gifted composer he received a basic grounding in the techniques of composition.

After his father's death in 1697, Handel continued his studies for a career in law, but by the time he was 17 he was an accomplished musician, a brilliant organist and harpsichordist, and had a number of compositions behind him. So when he entered the University of Halle he was at the same time appointed organist of the Domkirche in Halle. The composer Telemann was also a student at Halle and their friendship dates from this period.

Hamburg

In 1703, only a year after entering the University, he gave up his law studies and moved from Halle to the bustling commercial city of Hamburg. Unlike most German centres at that time, Hamburg was a free city, not dominated by a prince or ruler – and it had a public opera house. Handel made a living taking pupils and playing second violin and then harpsi-

Luca Carlevaris 'Arrival of the Fourth Earl of Manchester in Venice in 1707'. By courtesy of Birmingham Museums and Art Gallery

Georg Handel (above), father of the composer, hoped his son would have a legal career. Handel studied law for a year at the University of Halle and at the same time was organist at the Cathedral. In 1703 he gave up his studies and job to make his way in Hamburg (right).

BBC Hulton Picture Library

Archiv für Kunst und Geschichte

chord in the opera-house orchestra. He made many friends here, notably, Reinhard Keiser, the talented composer who directed the opera, and Johann Mattheson, a young composer and music commentator. Despite the fact that at one time Handel and Mattheson quarrelled, and even fought a duel, their friendship endured. Mattheson later recalled that Handel was a weak melodist, that he composed lengthy arias and interminable cantatas, but was a good writer of harmony and counterpoint. Mattheson also remarked that he found Handel to be a strong and independent character with a 'natural inclination to dry humour'.

Both young men applied for the post of organist at the nearby city of Lübeck. However, after visiting Lübeck it seems that both were put off by one of the conditions of the job: marriage to the unattractive daughter of the organist, Buxtehude.

Back in Hamburg, Handel began composing his first opera, *Almira,* which was enthusiastically received when performed in 1705. His second and third operas were less successful: the third was too long and had to be split into two operas, *Florindo* and *Daphne.* By the time they were produced in Hamburg Handel had gone to Italy, at the instigation of the son of the Grand Duke of Tuscany.

He arrived in Florence in the autumn of 1706 and

Handel aged 22 (above). He was 21 when he went to Italy in 1706. He spent three years there absorbing all that was on offer in a country where musical life flourished. When he returned to Germany he was widely recognized as one of the most gifted composers of the day.

travelled to Rome soon after. Here he quickly made important friends among the Roman aristocracy. His first oratorio (a musical setting of a sacred subject) was composed and performed in Rome in 1707, and by May 1707 he was in the employ of the Marquis Francesco Ruspoli, as household musician. His chief duty was to supply cantatas for the Marquis's weekly concerts. His largest work for Ruspoli was an oratorio, *La Resurrezione,* performed at Easter, 1708. He also wrote a great deal of church music for Ruspoli including a brilliant and imaginative setting of the *Dixit Dominus.*

As his reputation spread, he received invitations to all the main musical centres of Italy. At the end of 1709 he visited Venice, where his opera, *Agrippina,* received great acclaim and was performed no fewer than 27 times. His visit to Italy was successful on many levels, above all because he became so fluent in the Italian operatic style, but he also made a number of important contacts. One of these was Prince Ernst August of Hanover, the brother of the Elector of Hanover, Georg Ludwig, the future King George I of England. Another was the Duke of Manchester, the English ambassador to Venice.

Both men encouraged Handel to visit their respective countries, and when he left Italy in 1710, he went to Hanover as head of music at the Elector's

One of the influential people Handel met in Italy was the Duke of Manchester, whose splendid arrival in Venice is shown above. The Duke was the English Ambassador to Venice in 1707. He told Handel much about England and strongly encouraged him to come and see it for himself.

court. One of the conditions Handel made before he took up the post, was that he should be granted 12 months' leave to visit London, which even at this stage seemed to be the place which attracted him most. His employer raised no objections – after all, he knew he himself was likely to be going to London as King when Queen Anne died.

First visit to London

Handel's visit to London lasted eight months. He arrived in London late in 1710 and, probably because of his Hanoverian connections, was warmly received at Queen Anne's court where he gave at least one concert. However, his sights were set on the opera, and his first London opera, *Rinaldo,* was produced in February 1711. It was a huge success, despite the ridicule of critics who thought the idea of performing Italian opera in England absurd.

Handel directed all the performances from the harpsichord, and dazzled the audiences with the

Handel's royal employer, the Elector of Hanover, was crowned King George I of England and Scotland (left) in 1714 on the death of Queen Anne.

The London to which Handel was attracted was a place where people took a lively interest in enjoying themselves. A great cross-section of people spent their leisure time in the relaxed atmosphere of the city's many parks and gardens, as reflected by this painting.

Handel's compositions, like the Suites de Pieces pour le Clavecin *(below), were published by a variety of people, not always with his permission. In 1720 Handel obtained a 14-year copyright privilege, but as this gave him little protection against pirate publishers, he dropped it in 1724. His problems were not only with publishers: some professional musicians gave performances of his works without consulting or paying him. His most successful way of stopping this practice was to revise and enlarge the original scores and then give performance of the 'new' works.*

brilliance of his playing. During this visit to London he met the assistant manager of the opera, J. J. Heidegger and his niece, Mary Granville, then aged 10, who became a life-long friend and admirer. He also attended many concerts and performed regularly at private concerts, among them those given by Thomas Britton, a music-loving coal merchant.

The London opera season finished in June and Handel hastened back to Germany. Apart from some time in Halle, visiting his family, he spent 15 months working in Hanover producing chamber and orchestral works before returning to England. He had agreed with Prince Georg Ludwig, the Elector, that he would return to Hanover within a reasonable period of time, but he had been learning English and was greatly attracted by the musical opportunities offered in London, so it is likely that when he arrived in London in the autumn of 1712 he had every intention of settling there. In fact, he spent the next 47 years living in London.

In London, Handel quickly produced two new Italian operas: *Il pastor fido* in 1712 and *Teseo* early in 1713. He dedicated the libretto (the text of an opera, written usually by a commissioned librettist) of *Teseo* to the young Earl of Burlington, a leading patron of the arts. From 1713 to 1716 Handel lived in Burlington House in Piccadilly. Here the earl and his mother entertained many of the important literary figures of the day, including Alexander Pope and John Gay. Handel spent his days composing and in the evenings played for the Burlington guests. During this time he also composed a number of church works, including a *Te Deum* and *Jubilate* to celebrate the Peace of Utrecht. He also wrote a birthday ode for Queen Anne which was performed in 1713, her last birthday.

Queen Anne died in August 1714, and was succeeded by George I, the Elector of Hanover from whom Handel had played truant. Much has been written about Handel's truancy and the King's

supposed anger. One anecdote suggests that the *Water Music* was composed to pacify the monarch who, it is said, found himself being serenaded from a neighbouring barge during a water party on the Thames. Another story has it that the Italian violinist Geminiani helped restore Handel to favour by insisting that only Handel could accompany him when he played before the King.

In fact, George I was probably not in the least cross with Handel: within days of his arrival in London he heard some of Handel's music, and one of his first actions was to double Handel's salary as royal music master. Whether or not there was a water party with music in 1715, such an event did take place two years later and it was probably then that the well known *Water Music* was composed.

In 1716 Handel made a brief visit to Germany to see his family in Halle. He also went to Ansbach where he met an old University friend, J. C. Schmidt, and invited him back to London as his copyist and secretary. Schmidt, or Smith, as he soon became, and his son remained Handel's faithful friends and assistants to the end of his life, although there were times when Handel was not always well disposed to the elder Smith.

London becomes an opera centre

By the end of 1716 Handel was back in London supervising the revival of two of his operas. In the summer of 1717 he moved out of London to Edgware, when he became resident composer of the Earl of Carnarvon (later the Duke of Chandos), at his splendid country house, Cannons. Handel was there until 1720, during which time he composed 11 anthems for the chapel as well as two dramatic works: the pastoral serenade *Acis and Galatea,* and the first of his dramatic works on biblical subjects in English, a musical treatment of the story of Esther. There was no opportunity for writing opera at Cannons but it was still uppermost in Handel's mind.

Up to this time, though operas were frequently performed, no permanent opera centre existed in London. But many wealthy patrons of the arts were interested in creating one. Their discussions resulted in the establishment of the Royal Academy of Music, a commercial as well as artistic venture. The King was a patron and many leading noblemen, including Burlington, supported it. Handel was appointed the musical director and early in 1719 he went to the continent to sign up a team of singers. He made a brief stop in Halle (Bach went there to see him, but Handel left before he arrived!) but his main port of call was the court of Dresden where he persuaded several of the leading soloists to work in London.

Handel's career over the next few years reflects the ups and downs of opera in London and this subject is fully covered on pages 67–73.

Handel's activities from 1720 to 1728 centred around the King's Theatre in the Haymarket, which was the home of the Academy. During this time he composed a series of operas, including many of his finest works. In 1723 he moved into a handsome house in Brook Street, near Grosvenor Square, and in 1726 became a naturalized British subject. The

Handel lived at Burlington House (left) in Piccadilly from 1713 to 1716 as the guest of his friend, the young Earl of Burlington. Then aged 18, the Earl was already one of the leading patrons of art and literature in London.

A caricature (above) of some of the resident singers engaged by Handel for the Royal Academy of Music. Seen here (left to right) are Senesino, Cuzzoni and Berenstadt.

The first opera Handel wrote for his London début was Rinaldo (top centre, painting of Rinaldo under the spell of Almirena by Tiepolo). The scenario was drafted by Aaron Hill, a dramatist and the manager of the Queen's Theatre, Haymarket where the opera was first performed on 24 February 1711. It was a huge success and received a further 15 performances during the season.

following year he was commissioned to write anthems for George II's coronation in Westminster Abbey. One of these anthems, *Zadok the Priest*, has been performed at every coronation since then.

Collapse of the Academy
However, not everything went smoothly for the Royal Academy of Music. Its directors were often at odds with each other and there were increasing financial problems. There were scandals and public scenes involving some of the singers, which damaged the prestige of the Academy and the audiences frequently behaved badly — their cat calls and disturbances hardly added to the atmosphere. As a result, the Royal Academy of Music ran out of money in the summer of 1728.

Handel did not suffer much for the demise of the Academy, since he was a salaried employee not the proprietor. He also received salaries from the Royal family and since 1723 had been employed as a composer to the Chapel Royal. However, he still wished to have his operas performed, so he entered into a contract with the former opera house manager, J. J. Heidegger and the Director of the Academy agreed to let the King's Theatre to him for five years. Some of his new operas met with mild success though his singers did not always impress the audience.

Handel's last year of tenure at the King's Theatre saw the formation by a group of noblemen and musicians of a rival opera company called the Opera of the Nobility. Heidegger let the King's Theatre to his new group in 1734, and Handel transferred his own opera company to a newer theatre in Covent Garden. In the summer he visited Oxford (he was offered a doctorate in music, but declined to accept it) and gave oratorios including the new *Athalia*, in the Sheldonian theatre.

He continued to direct his energies and his genius, primarily towards opera and early 1735 saw the production of two of his supreme operas, *Ariodante* and *Alcina*. It was not until 1737 that the crash came, and both Handel's opera company and the Opera of

John Christopher Smith (above) or Johann Christoph Schmidt as he was originally known, was a friend from Handel's university days. In 1716 Handel persuaded him to leave Ansbach, where he was involved in the wool trade, and come to London to work for him as copyist and secretary.

the Nobility closed — financially devastated by lack of popular support.

Just before this, Handel had suffered what might have been a stroke or an attack of severe rheumatism. Partly paralysed, he made a journey to Aix-la-Chapelle, to take the baths.

By October he made an amazing recovery and within a couple of weeks was at work on a new opera. His old impresario colleague, Heidegger, who had briefly defected to the Nobility, was now back at the King's Theatre and he engaged Handel as composer and Director. However, although Handel composed

The portly Handel (above) was known for his vast appetite, but the cartoon (left) by Goupy upset him. Handel is depicted as a pig, because after a frugal meal together, during which Handel told Goupy of his financial difficulties, he saw Handel drinking Burgundy on his own! Goupy left the house angrily and published this cartoon a few days later.

of six had been published in 1738), were intended for performance between the acts of oratorios. Indeed, Handel's playing of organ concertos became one of the attractions at his oratorio performances from this time on.

Dublin and Messiah

Handel's last operas, given in the 1740–41 season, were total failures and from then on he withdrew from the opera scene. His English works given about the same time had scarcely more success so it was not surprising that rumours became rife that he was planning to leave England. Whether Handel intended to leave England or not, an invitation from Dublin, to give performances came opportunely, and during summer, 1741, he prepared himself by writing a new work. He had, it seems, been asked to prepare a work for a performance in aid of Dublin charities and for this he chose a sacred topic: the coming of the Messiah. He also composed *Samson,* a new oratorio partly based on the poems of Milton.

Handel arrived in Dublin in November 1741. Just before Christmas, he embarked upon his first six-concert subscription series which were greatly enjoyed. In a letter home to Charles Jennens, the man who had compiled the texts for *Messiah* and other works, Handel expressed his delight with his Dublin success. However the climax of his trip to Dublin came on 13 April 1742 with the first performance of *Messiah.*

Handel's activities at the Queen's Theatre (later King's) ended in 1734. He moved to a new theatre (above) in Covent Garden managed by John Rich. An organ belonging to Handel (seen in the picture) was installed in the theatre and in his will he left the instrument to Rich, but it was destroyed in a fire in 1808.

a few more operas he was more interested in writing oratorios – which had a more appreciative audience than opera. His public, which now included members of the middle classes, was not keen on the 'exotic and irrational' notion of opera in a foreign language and preferred instead to hear familiar biblical stories in English and to be uplifted by the power of Handel's music. In response to this demand, he performed *Saul* and *Israel in Egypt* in 1739 (the first was a success, the second failed). That year he also composed the famous Twelve Grand Concertos for strings, op. 6. These, like the organ concertos (a set

Oratorios in London

Handel was back in London at the end of summer 1742, with a welcome success behind him after the tribulations of the preceding years. From now on his life took a more regular pattern. He had given up opera (though he had tempting offers to return to it), and now pursued an idea that may have been suggested by the success of his subscription series in Dublin. He directed almost all his energies towards organizing an oratorio season, each Lent, at Covent Garden. That of 1743, with *Samson* as its main attraction, was a success, although the inclusion of *Messiah* did it little good – London audiences were suspicious of the idea of an oratorio with biblical words in a theatre. In fact, *Messiah* became popular in London only in 1750, when Handel started performing it (as he had in Dublin) in aid of charity.

The pattern of performances was established, but the pattern of the music to be performed was not. For the 1744 season, Handel included a new work that was neither oratorio nor opera; *Semele,* designed for concert rather than stage performance, and on a classical rather than Biblical theme – and a highly profane one at that, dealing with the love affair between Jupiter and Semele. It was unsuccessful; the new audience must have been puzzled by it, for it offered none of the enlightment or moral uplift that they had come to expect. He presented the same formula the next year, with *Hercules,* another classical drama; both this and *Semele* (which was revived the next season) were poorly received, and Handel almost had to cancel his season. His new biblical oratorio, *Belshazzar,* was also received with indifference. This particular season was given at the King's, rather than at Covent Garden; perhaps these works' limited appeal to the opera audiences had something to do with their relative failure.

But things improved. In 1746, circumstances were on Handel's side: the 1745 rebellion had been firmly put down, and the nation was in patriotic mood – and

the mood is caught in Handel's *Occasional Oratorio* and his *Judas Maccabaeus,* the new works of 1746 and 1747.

Encouraged by their success, Handel seems to have been in good spirits and full of creative energy in the late 1740s. He wrote two new oratorios in each of the summers of 1747 and 1748, those of the latter year, *Solomon* and *Susanna,* being among his finest works. 1748 was also the year of the treaty of Aix-la-Chapelle, which ratified the succession of Maria Theresa, to the Austro-Hungarian throne. As this was settled in favour of his allies, George II decided it ought to be publicly celebrated; Handel was invited to write the music to go with a firework display – the Music for the Royal Fireworks.

With a substantial oratorio repertoire built up, Handel, now over 60, eased up somewhat on composition. The new oratorio in 1750 was *Theodora,* which had only modest success – Handel is reported as saying, ironically, that the music sounded better in an empty hall.

Ill-health and failing sight

In summer 1750, Handel made his last journey to Europe. We do not know where he went: he may have visited friends and relatives in Halle. In 1751, back in London at work on a new oratorio, *Jephtha,* he began to be seriously troubled by his failing sight; he wrote into the score that he was forced to stop work, just at the passage where the chorus sing 'How dark, O Lord, are Thy decrees, all hid from mortal sight'. *Jephtha* was, however, completed, and had its first performance the following year; it was his last complete original composition.

In 1759, he was still able to give an oratorio season; but his health was failing. Five days after the season ended, in April, he added a final codicil to his will, including a request for burial in Westminster Abbey. He died three days later. At his funeral 3,000 Londoners were present and the funeral anthem was sung by the choirs of the Chapels Royal, St Paul's and Westminster Abbey.

Many contemporaries left accounts of events in Handel's life. He was a big man with a vast appetite; he was quick to anger and impatient, but witty too. He never married and although he was a social man with many friends in the upper strata of London society, there are gaps in our knowledge of his personal relationships. Perhaps it is best to look to the warmth, vivacity and drama of his music to appreciate the sort of man he was.

Handel's last codicil to his will provided for a sum 'not exceeding Six Hundred Pounds' for his own monument, by Roubiliac, in Westminster Abbey.

Handel took the waters at many spa towns including Aix-la-Chapelle, Bath and Cheltenham. The last spa town he visited was Tunbridge Wells (above) in August and September 1758. He made plans to return to Bath in April 1759 but was too weak to make the journey. He took to his bed and died on 14 April in his house in Brook Street.

COMPOSER'S LIFE
'Italian bondage'

By training and temperament, Handel was a composer of theatrical music and his determination to bring Italian opera to London was a constant and financially ruinous pre-occupation.

From its 16th century use as an extravagant courtly entertainment Italian opera grew in stature until, by the 18th century, it had become the predominant musical influence in Europe. Handel himself was deeply indebted to its rich musical traditions and exploited its potential to the full. The rich costumes (such as shown right) and elaborate staging of Italian opera did much initially to attract London audiences to the genre.

The story of Handel in the early part of the 18th century is closely entwined with the story of opera in London. For it was under his personal and artistic influence that this musical form – banned by the Puritans in the mid-17th century, and scorned as 'foreign' even 40 years later – achieved any popularity. So determined were Handel's efforts that London in the 1720s became the operatic centre of Europe, with the best composers, best singers and best scenic designers. But the public's support was never without reservation and audiences' interests passing, and in spite of Handel's persistence with the form, it eventually faded from view. Nevertheless opera remained dear to his heart, and comprised an important part of his musical career.

Italian opera in London

When Handel first arrived in London from Germany in late 1710, Italian opera was just becoming popular, both with the middle-class paying public and most, if not all, of the aristocracy. This is not to say it received universal acclaim as evidenced by Dr Johnson's remark – possibly after seeing *Almahide,* London's first Italian opera totally in Italian – that it was 'an exotick (sic) and irrational entertainment'. London's first opera house had been in existence for five years, and many theatres mounted operatic productions. The soil seemed fertile for Italian opera – or so Handel thought.

But what was Italian opera in Handel's time? In many respects it differed from opera as we know it today. Developed by Italian masters, opera was based on stories that were taken from mythology or history. Preceding each opera was a *sinfonia,* an overture generally of three or four movements, none of which represented the music heard in the ensuing drama. Action – other than in the 'spectacular elements' and the ballets and other acts that were included as diversions – was severely limited.

There were few duets or trios and no true choruses at all. Dialogue between characters occurred in *recitative* speech but at a musical pitch; at dramatic moments it would be backed by the full orchestra. The arias or songs – and each full-scale opera would have about 30 – would be performed by soloists who merely stood and sang – embellishment was not the fashion. When finished, they left the stage, returning briefly for applause. Scene changes were made in full view of the audience, the music covering most of the sound. The music itself was Italian in style – thoughtful and melodic; the manner of singing was declamatory.

The Italian singers' virtuosity took pride of place, and it was the function of the composer and librettist to supply them with songs which could best display their voices. Arias were doled out in proportion to the artiste's importance, with the main singers – the leading lady or *prima donna,* the soprano and the *primo uomo* or leading man, who was usually a *castrato* – in theory receiving the share due to them, and most complained vociferously if deprived.

Shows of artistic temperament were displayed on-stage and off, with catcalls and orange throwing not unheard of. The somewhat circus-like atmosphere was mirrored by the behaviour of the audience who, in fully lit theatres, became a law unto themselves. Indeed during performances members of the audience would chat to their neighbours, drift off, go onstage, have a meal, play cards and carry on flirtations. Opera was a 'cultural' experience, but first and foremost was also a social occasion!

The King's Theatre Haymarket (above) was the chosen location for a Royal Academy of Music founded by King George I to promote Italian opera in London. Its early days were marked by a series of triumphs, but within ten years, the Academy was forced to close due to lack of public interest.

Undeterred by the changing tides of fortune, Handel transferred his operatic efforts to the theatre at Covent Garden (right). Not even the magnificent organ, central stage or the host of theatrical devices he employed could save his sinking fortunes, however, and the few full houses he did attract were rowdy and unappreciative!

A portrait of Handel painted around 1714 (left) reflects the comfortable style of living he enjoyed as a guest of the influential Lord Burlington. From 1713–1716, Handel stayed at Burlington House, composing by day and entertaining visitors by night. He successfully completed a number of operas and two of them – Teseo and Amadigi di Gaula – are dedicated to his generous host.

Early years

This then was the operatic tradition that Handel brought with him on his first visit to London, following his three year sojourn in Italy. While there he had become acquainted with some of the great operatic composers, and had written four operas, two of which – *Rodrigo,* first performed in Florence in 1706, and *Agrippina,* first performed in Venice in 1709 – were great successes.

Immediately he became immersed in London's opera world, making many useful contacts of potential patrons and impressarios, including the Swiss J. J. Heidegger, who was later to become a close business associate. While on this eight month leave from his employer, the Elector of Hanover, Georg Ludwig, the future King George I of England, he wrote the opera *Rinaldo,* which was based on the story of the Crusades. Although he incorporated some arias previously composed in Italy, his librettist, Giacomo Rossi, spread the word that Handel had composed the opera in two weeks – an awesome feat. Performed at the Queen's Theatre on 24 February 1711, *Rinaldo* was a huge success, although Addison and Steele, writing in *The Spectator,* panned the production, particularly for its use of live sparrows to lend realism to the Mediterranean grove in the story. Their criticism may have been sour grapes: Addison had recently had an English operatic failure and Steele had shares in the ordinary theatre. Handel, however, buoyed by his success, strengthened his resolve to return to London and set the opera world alight.

In 1712 Handel, then aged 27, did return and very soon after he began a three year residence at Burlington House, the home of Lord Burlington. There he met his host's influential friends, including the dramatist John Gay, whose own work was to presage Handel's operatic death knell.

During the next four years Handel wrote four more operas, including *Il pastor fido* (1712) and *Teseo* (1713). The former, which once more contained revised previous compositions, was a financial disaster – the Queen's Theatre manager, who had been particularly stingy in purchasing costumes and scenery, having absconded with the takings on the second night. The only bonus was that Handel's friend Heidegger became the theatre's manager, and this played an important part in Handel's opera career. *Teseo (Theseus),* which was

Alessandro Scarlatti (left) was a leading figure in the Neapolitan Opera School in Italy, and an associate of Handel's during his youthful days in Venice. There is nothing to suggest that they kept in touch when Handel came to England, but it is likely that he kept an eager eye out for news of Scarlatti's latest works – he was certainly not above adapting his musical ideas for his own operatic efforts!

Italian-style opera, supported by the Royal Academy, introduced new composers to London to augment Handel's works. One of the most popular was Bononcini (right), who attracted keen but partisan support from London's roisterous opera-goers.

A biting caricature of Italianate operas appeared in 1730. It showed the celebrated performers Cuzzoni and Farinelli singing a duet, with the impresario Heidegger seated behind them. According to a contemporary, 'it was printed in honour and glory of that great band of rogues – the singers'.

adapted from a French libretto, proved to be a great success. The spectacular production had a 'variety of Dancing and a great many Scenes and Machines' to produce special effects. Unfortunately, difficulties in maintaining the machines, the illness of the soloist, an unusually warm spring and the Jacobite rebellion all conspired to its premature closure.

In 1716 Handel briefly visited his friends and relatives in Germany, then returned to London to supervise the revival of two of his operas. In the summer of 1717 he moved to Edgware, and became resident composer to the Earl of Caernarvon (later the Duke of Chandos). During the next three years he composed only non-operatic works – in fact no Italian operas were formed in London at all between 1717 and 1720. However the form was still uppermost in Handel's mind and events were to come about which would allow his return to opera.

Handel and the Royal Academy

Between 1718 and 1719 a party of nobles under the patronage of the King decided to found an Academy to promote Italian opera in London. The funds for this venture – called the Royal Academy of Music – were raised by subscription: £200 bought a permanent ticket, and in all £20,000 was subscribed. The King's Theatre – formerly the Queen's – was taken over. In 1720 Handel was appointed musical director and Heidegger the manager.

Immediately Handel was dispatched abroad to engage the finest singers in Europe – English voices were not seen as being up to the demands of the Italian operatic style. Giovanni Battista Bononcini,

Thou tunefull Scarecrow, & thou warbling Bird,
No shelter for your Notes, these lands afford
This Town protects no more thi Sing Song Strain
Whilst Balls & Masquerades Triumphant Reign
Sooner than midnight revels ere should fail
And ore Ridottos Harmony prevail,
That Cap (a refuge once) my Head shall Grace
And save from ruin this Harmonious face

Nicolo Porpora (above), the renowned Italian composer, arrived in London in 1733 to become musical director of the so-called Opera of the Nobility – a company set up in competition with Handel's.

Lincoln's Inn Fields (below) was the elegant setting for a political satire, The Beggar's Opera, *that drove another nail into the coffin of Italian-style opera.*

one of the contributors to *Almahide* and a great operatic composer, was approached. A number of leading singers, including several of the best contemporary *castrati,* were signed up.

The grand opening of the Academy was on 2 April 1720. It featured the opera *Numitore* by Giovanni Porta (from which Handel borrowed some ideas, two decades later, for his oratorio *Samson*); a resounding success, it re-established Italian opera in London.

Four weeks later Handel's own *Radamisto* was performed to rapturous acclaim. The cast consisted of only seven players – fortuitously as the company's major stars, the castrati Senesino and Serselli, had not yet arrived from abroad. The libretto was an adaptation from an early source by Nicola Haym, one of Handel's most-used collaborators during this period.

But all did not bode well. In the autumn of 1720 Bononcini arrived in London and was engaged, along with the cellist Filippo Amadei, as a composer to the Academy. Bononcini's first production, *Astarto,* was an immediate success, running for longer than any of Handel's previous operatic productions. However when their jointly composed opera *Muzio Scevola* was produced in early 1721, the critics made it plain that they thought Handel's contribution by far the better. Further productions by both composers, however, again resulted in those by Bononcini running for longer.

Inevitably Handel and Bononcini became rivals and they, in turn, became the focus of bitter rivalry between factions of supporters, who became increasingly vocal and disruptive during per-

formances. The pampered and temperamental soloists – difficult to live with at the best of times – also began to take sides, waxing even more capricious than usual and using the threat of transferring allegiance as much as possible.

In the Academy's third season Bononcini's operas consistently had longer runs, and to boost attendances at his own productions, Handel went so far as altering his composing style towards Bononcini's simpler and more memorable melodies. He could not, however, change his artistic and dictatorial temperament, and he began to be involved in unseemly public wrangles with the resident librettist Paoli Rolli (who was temporarily dismissed) and with some of the *castrati,* including Senesino, whom he had clashed with before.

Matters soon got out of hand. When the celebrated soprano Francesca Cuzzoni arrived to take up her post towards the end of 1722, she became convinced that what was to prove the show-stopping first aria in Handel's new opera, *Ottone,* did not give her voice sufficient exposition. She only conceded to sing it when Handel stated that he would throw her out of a window if she continued to refuse. On another occasion, a Scots tenor became upset by Handel's accompaniment on the harpsichord, and threatened to jump on the instrument and break it. Handel's laconic reply was to ask for enough warning to sell tickets for such a performance as, he said, he was certain 'that more people would come to see you jump than to hear you sing'!

Ottone proved very successful, and this elevated Handel's stock above Bononcini's once more – to the raucous annoyance of Bononcini's supporters. Most of the audience, though, could hardly tell the music of the two composers apart. Indeed, wrote the Manchester diarist, poet and hymn-writer John Byrom:

'Some say, compar'd to Bononcini,
That Mynheer Handel's but a ninny;
Others aver, that he to Handel
Is scarcely fit to hold a Candle:
Strange that this Difference there should be
'Twixt Tweedle-dum and Tweedle-dee!'

In 1724 Handel went on to produce two more successes – *Giulio Cesare in Egitto (Julius Caesar in Egypt)* with Francesca Cuzzoni as an acclaimed Cleopatra and the *castrato* Senesino as Caesar, and *Tamerlano (Tamburlaine).* The following year he produced *Rodelinda* – another success, with Cuzzoni's silk costume for the eponymous heroine creating a new fashion. The librettist for all three was again Nicola Haym who, under Handel's close supervision, adapted older Italian librettos to London taste.

The decline

But all was not well. In 1726, the Academy found itself paying enormous sums of money either to secure or retain the services of its soloists; increasingly this led to financial difficulties. A particularly large fee – possibly as much as £2500 – was paid to the soprano Faustina Bordoni to join the company. Signoras Bordoni and Cuzzoni disliked each other on sight, and in his operas thereafter Handel had to be extremely careful that both were given equivalent but different roles. This he did with his next two operas – *Alessandro* (1726) and *Admeto* (1727) – both of which were well-received. But at a Bononcini opera later that year the two

ladies – urged on by reprobates in the audience – actually set about each other on stage, to the horror of all present, including the Prince of Wales.

Coupled with the high overheads, the Academy's receipts were down as too few people were renewing their subscriptions. Italian opera was fast losing ground to alternative diversions in London.

The final straw was the opening of the innovatory entertainment that was John Gay's *The Beggar's Opera* in January 1728 in Lincoln's Inn Fields. People flocked to see this new satire on the Prime Minister, Sir Robert Walpole, and to enjoy the songs (including some by Purcell, Handel and Bononcini), rather than to see either of Handel's operas for that year, *Siroe* and *Tolomeo* (*Ptolemy*, which contained the well-known aria *Silent Worship*). On 1 June, the

In keeping with the heroic style of many operas in the 18th century, composers often drew inspiration from such sources as Greek and Roman history. Handel composed three such operas based on the works of the famous librettist and poet Metastasio – Siroe (above), Poro and Ezio – and each was characterized by lofty ideals and rather stiff characterization.

Academy closed and its company dispersed.

Italian operas were evidently no longer popular but this did not deter Handel. With the agreement of the Academy directors, he and Heidegger took out a five year lease on the King's Theatre and borrowed their scenery, costumes and machines. Again subscriptions were used to fund the company, with Handel being paid a salary as before, this time £1000. Both principals then left for Europe to find and bring back new talent: Handel travelled through Venice, Rome, Halle (to see his mother, who died the following year), Hanover and Hamburg. He returned to London on 29 June with singers who, except for the distinguished but aged *castrato* Bernacchi, had never sung on the English stage before.

Handel composed two operas for the first season – *Lotario* in December 1729 and *Partenope* in February 1730, where he changed his style from heroic drama to ironic comedy; both were flops. This may have been due to Bernacchi's presence and so at great expense he replaced Bernacchi with the ever-popular Senesino, who he recalled from Italy. As in other instances in his operatic career, he fell back on revivals for the second season, including *Rinaldo*

and *Rodelinda;* his one new opera, *Poro,* met only with modest success. Indeed in the third season the revivals continued to be more popular than his new operas, *Ezio* and *Sosarme* (in *Sosarme* many of the recitatives were printed in the programme and not performed on stage because the audience found them especially boring); both of these operas were disasters.

In 1732 an event occurred that was to change Handel's musical career. His oratorio *Esther* was given a private performance, and was greeted with the success accorded to his early operas. Unfortunately, the public performances were marred by the raucous Bononcini fan club and this response should, perhaps, have prompted Handel to look for a different musical form. However, Handel, as ever, remained steadfast in his resolve to continue with opera.

Rivalry and composition

Handel was now being urged by his friends to abandon Italian opera, or to compromise by writing English versions. 'Deliver us from our Italian bondage,' wrote Aaron Hill, the theatre manager of

A delightful study of 'a musical party in the garden of Kew Palace' (left) shows Handel's young pupils, Frederick the Prince of Wales and his three sisters, in harmonious mood. In later years, however, a note of discord entered their relationship: Frederick became patron of Handel's great rival the Opera of the Nobility.

Handel's last operatic success, Alcina, starred the vivacious dancer Marie Sallé (below). At first well received in London, she 'composed a ballet in which she cast herself for the role of Cupid and took upon herself to dance it in male attire'. The result was a fiasco and Sallé fled home to Paris to recover!

But neither this nor the rival Opera of the Nobility came up with a hit. By the time Handel and Heidegger moved out of the King's Theatre – and the Opera of the Nobility moved in – the popularity of Italian opera in London was at its lowest ebb. In his new venue, the recently constructed playhouse in Covent Garden, Handel tried all the tricks he kenw – cutting the recitatives altogether, reviving old operas, interpolating novelty acts, creating operas round a French ballet company, even satirizing his own previous successes – in order to get the audiences to return. It was a forlorn effort; he only achieved sporadic and temporary success.

Alcina, his last operatic success, featured the ballet-dancer Marie Sallé, who had first been engaged for performances of *Rinaldo* 17 years earlier when she was only 10 years old. With her revealing costume she first caused a sensation and then disruption in the audiences; after 18 performances, the later ones punctuated with hisses, the poor lady fled and never came back.

Although the two rival companies staged a few further operas – Handel wrote no fewer than three in 1737, whereas Porpora returned to Italy, defeated – all were utter failures. In 1741 both companies closed signalling opera's final demise. Within the year, however, Handel's fortunes brightened considerably – he wrote the *Messiah* and re-established himself as England's major composer.

the old Queen's Theatre, 'and demonstrate that English is soft enough for opera . . . .' Handel ignored his advice, conceding only to write oratorios in English. His opera *Orlando* (January 1733) was put on with considerable spectacle, but it was not as successful with the public as was his oratorio *Deborah* performed only two months later.

During this time serious disagreements again arose between Handel and the company, with the result that almost all of the company either walked out or were sacked and, in retaliation, founded their own company, under the patronage of certain nobles; they called themselves the Opera of the Nobility. Mostly Italian, the performers included the public's favourite, Senesino. The leading Italian composer, Nicolo Porpora, was appointed musical director (Haydn was at one time Porpora's pupil and, surprisingly, his valet). The company's principal patron was the Prince of Wales, while Handel's, as always, was the King.

Competition for the dwindling London audience was increased to the point of ferocity. Handel, who still had the final year of his lease at the King's Theatre to fulfil, gamely tried with a new company.

Listener's guide

Any analysis of the life and times of a great composer cannot ignore his music, and this section examines in detail some of Handel's greatest and best-known works: Messiah, the Water Music and his Music for the Royal Fireworks. Together with sections on specific aspects of musical development of relevance to the works under discussion (for example, the development of the oratorio and the cantata), the descriptions of the pieces of music can be read independently as an examination of Handel's musical achievements. However, for the fullest appreciation of this great composer's music, the programme notes are better read before going to a live performance or while listening to the recorded music. Suggestions for further listening are given in the text, and the Bibliography and the short descriptions of the lives and works of Handel's contemporaries on page 110 suggest other areas of study.

LISTENER'S GUIDE

LISTENER'S GUIDE

Messiah

Handel based his enthralling and magnificent Messiah on the dramatic story of Christ as told in the Bible – a glorious challenge the composer triumphantly rose to.

Handel received the libretto (text) of *Messiah* in July 1741 after an unhappy opera season. His last two operas, *Imeneo* and *Deidamia,* are both delightful, but had both failed miserably. Their lack of success marked the end of his long career as an opera composer with over 40 lyric dramas to his credit. It was inevitable then, that Handel should cast around for a new text to set, modelled on his most recent and successful experiments with oratorios (dramatic musical settings of biblical texts) and odes. The libretto for his last ode, *L'Allegro, il Penseroso, ed il Moderato* (1740) had been prepared by

Charles Jennens, Handel's friend, and the librettist of the epic oratorios *Saul* (1739) and later *Belshazzar* (1744). In *Saul* and *Belshazzar* he provided Handel with towering conceptions of national struggles and finely drawn characterizations. In *L'Allegro* he rearranged two separate poems by Milton into a charming musical debate between a pensive man and a cheerful man. This 'paste and scissors' composition proved a marvellous spur to Handel's imagination, while Milton's rich imagery allowed him full scope for orchestral colour.

In *Messiah,* Jennens again tried the same basic technique that he had employed in

L'Allegro, but used the resounding phrases of the King James' translation of the Bible. With the exception of Shakespeare, where else could Jennens have found a greater inspiration for Handel?

Jennens' concern in *Messiah* was to outline the life of Christ for the listener, but with little reference to direct narrative. Instead, he used a few familiar quotations, and a few Gospel texts, but the greater part

The Messiah, *in its depiction of the life of Christ, is able to evoke intense religious feelings as can this ceiling painting showing God, the Son and the Holy Spirit surrounded by angels and saints.*

Although unpopular because of his vanity and obstinacy, Charles Jennens (above) was a gifted man who stunned the public with the libretto he wrote for Handel's Messiah – (photograph of original score on the right). Jennens' temperament was the cause of a temporary rift in his friendship with the composer.

of the libretto is drawn from obscure prophecies and 'unpopular' books of the Old Testament. The resulting three-part structure gives a wonderful sense of drama by its perfect progression from prophecy through suffering to fulfilment and, ultimately, triumph.

Handel was obviously delighted. In one of his customary spells of 'white hot' creativity, he began setting the text on 22 August 1741. He finished it on 14 Sep-

Susanna Cibber, the famous singer/actress was one of the female soloists who sang at the opening performance of the Messiah in Dublin.

tember. This in itself would seem amazing, but to then continue with the three long acts of *Samson* which he finished on 29 October, is little short of miraculous. Nevertheless, there is no reason to think that it was an example of direct divine inspiration. The popular image of Handel displayed on his tomb in Westminster Abbey may satisfy a sentimental response to the composer. It shows him holding the music of 'I know that my Redeemer liveth' from the *Messiah* while angels hover above and behind him. It is more reasonable to think of him as a musical genius who, like Tchaikovsky, could describe his daily creative process with the rather cynical phrase, 'The Muses have learned to be on time.'

First performance in Dublin

It was sometime during the summer of 1741 that Handel decided to accept an invitation to visit Dublin to perform a series of his works. A similar trip to Oxford earlier in his life had proved invigorating, and since his career in London seemed to be in the doldrums, Dublin appeared an attractive prospect. As his first biographer, Capt. John Mainwaring put it:

Dublin has always been famous for the gaiety and splendour of its court, the opulence and spirit of its principal inhabitants, the valour of its military, and the genius of its learned men. Where such things were held in esteem he rightly reckoned that he could not better pave the way to his success, than by setting out with a striking instance and public act of

generosity and benevolence. The first step that he made, was to perform his Messiah *for the benefit of the city-prison. Such a design drew together not only all the lovers of Music, but all the friends of humanity. There was a peculiar propriety in this design from the subject of the Oratorio itself; and there was a peculiar grace in it from the situation of Handel's affairs.*

In fact, Handel did not present *Messiah* until the end of his season in Dublin, but hints (in those days called 'puffs') were regularly dropped in the press. A public rehearsal on 8 April, a few days before the first performance on 12 April, seemed to guarantee its success. An audience of 700 pressed into the Music Hall in Fishamble Street, (designed to accommodate 600) so that Faulkner's *Dublin Journal* on 10 April felt obliged to request:

Many Ladies and Gentlemen who are well-wishers to this Noble and Grand Charity for which this Oratorio was composed, request it as a Favour, that the Ladies who honour this Performance with their Presence would be pleased to come without Hoops, as it will greatly increase the Charity, by making Room for more company.

It was presumably a similar motive that led to a later demand: 'The Gentlemen are desired to come without their Swords.'

The cast of *Messiah* included men from both cathedrals in Dublin, taking alto, tenor and bass parts. The female soloists included an Italian soprano, Signora Avoglio and the distinguished Susanna Maria Cibber, sister of the composer Thomas Arne, who became associated with the beautiful aria 'I know that my Redeemer liveth.' Handel's choice of an actress as well as a great singer for this solo part in *Messiah* may indicate the stress he desired to be placed upon the beauties of the text. Certainly, Mrs Cibber was long associated with this song and was able to move her audience deeply.

It is interesting to note that Jonathan Swift, the famous Dean of St Patrick's Cathedral and author of *Gulliver's Travels,* initially opposed the use of his choristers by Handel for his performance, but eventually allowed them to take part.

Handel was delighted with his success in Ireland, and his happiness is expressed in a wonderfully jaunty letter to Jennens in December 1741.

. . . the Performance was received with a general Approbation. The Musick sounds delightfully in this charming Room,

Although successful in Dublin, the Messiah got off to a slow start in England, but grew in popularity when Handel started performing it for charity. His favourite charity was the Foundling Hospital, and he frequently gave concerts in its chapel (below).

which puts me in such Spirits (and my Health being so good) that I exert my self on my Organ with more than usual Success . . . I cannot sufficiently express the kind treatment I receive here, but the Politeness of this generous Nation cannot be unknown to You, so I let You judge of the satisfaction I enjoy, passing my time with Honour, profit and pleasure.

He remained in Dublin for ten months before returning to London.

Messiah's growing popularity

The first London performance of *Messiah* in 1743 did not go well. Religious opposition to a scriptural libretto being performed by Handel's actress-singer in the Covent Garden theatre meant that Handel's advertisements for the work did not even mention its title. It was simply referred to as 'A New Sacred Oratorio.' The real success of that season was undoubtedly *Samson,* in Handel's more usual heroic dramatic style.

It was not until 1750 that Handel began giving *Messiah* in Lent season at Covent Garden and then repeating it as a charity concert in the chapel of the Foundling Hospital in Coram's Fields. This estab-

lishment still operates, although the chapel was destroyed in the 1920s. It was founded by a retired sea-captain named Thomas Coram who persuaded Handel, Hogarth, and many others to help in his great project. Handel's concerts both ensured its early financial stability and gave a backdrop to *Messiah* closely allied to its origins in Dublin. By the time Handel died, *Messiah* had become immensely popular.

After the composer's death, an amazing transformation took place. Handel, the great life-loving and genial liberal was 'institutionalized.' Performances of *Messiah* grew in number. So did the forces used to perform it. This meant that the speed of performance had to be slowed down and the shining orchestration became muddied by too many instruments. More often than not, the work was referred to as *The Messiah* and was treated like some addendum to Anglican worship and thus the property of the State Church. Handel, who wrote for Catholic and Protestant, Jew and Christian, would have hated this hide-bound tradition. It is the ultimate irony that the man whose theatrical oratorios incensed the Bishop of London should, until recently, have had his music played solely in churches.

It is worth noting some of the differences between an oratorio performance in Handel's day and most performances today. Firstly, Handel's chorus was all male, the soprano and alto parts being taken by boy trebles and counter-tenors. Female soloists were used, of course, but they and all the soloists were expected to participate in the choruses. Since the chorus remained standing throughout, there were no gaps between arias and choruses to deflate dramatic tension and cripple pace. Each act was much more musically unified. There was no conductor: Handel led from the keyboard and used musicians he respected and trusted. His orchestra numbered about 35 and his chorus 19. Since the five soloists joined in the choruses, the balance between singers and players was equal, especially in regard to the strings. Tasteful ornamentation was encouraged in the repeats. How different these performing forces were compared to the hordes of 19th-century musicians lumbering through elephantine versions of *Messiah* in the Crystal Palace!

Programme notes

Jennens divided his libretto into three sections, usually referred to as 'Nativity', 'Passion' and 'Redemption'. The first part deals with the prophecies concerning the coming of the birth of Christ. The second part tells of the suffering and torment of the Lamb of God, and the spread of the Gospel. The third part considers the redemption of sinful man, and the promise of eternal salvation. Handel, a master of dramatic oratorio, visualized each scene as he was writing it. He said, while composing the famous 'Hallelujah' chorus that it was as if he saw 'God on his throne and all his angels round him'. It is this quality which makes *Messiah* Handel's masterpiece.

Part the First

'Comfort ye, My people – Ev'ry valley' (tenor)
Comfort ye, comfort ye My people
saith your God.
Speak ye comfortably to Jerusalem,
and cry unto her, that her warfare is
accomplished,
that her iniquity is pardoned.
The voice of him that crieth in the wilderness;
prepare ye the way of the Lord;
make straight in the desert a highway
for our God.
Isaiah 40:1–3

Ev'ry valley shall be exalted,
and ev'ry mountain and hill made low;
the crooked straight and the rough places plain.
Isaiah 40:4

In an accompanied recitative (a vocal composition which imitates the patterns of speech and, in this context, serves as narrative) the tenor proclaims the biblical prophecy which announced the arrival of the Messiah. The gentle repeated figure of the strings creates an atmosphere of calm

contentment which is reinforced by the tenor's soft call to comfort. The music rises on the word 'cry' as the singer prepares for the manifestation of the Lord. A declamatory passage gives God's call prominence and leads into the following *aria*.

Handel set 'Ev'ry valley' as a spirited tenor aria which contains a wonderful musical depiction of the valleys being lifted up and the mountains being laid low. Similarly, a wavering string and vocal figure represents the rough and crooked places which are then made 'plain' or level by means of a long sustained note.

Example 1

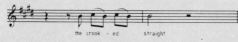

the crook - ed straight

'And the Glory of the Lord' (chorus)
And the Glory of the Lord shall be revealed,
and all flesh shall see it together:
for the mouth of the Lord hath spoken it.
Isaiah 40:5

A lively chorus follows, cheerfully singing their message and placing much emphasis on the word 'Glory' – a favourite Handelian concept. Confirmation of God's intent is voiced by the repetition of sustained notes by the lower voices: the tenors and basses. Handel's writing tends to be 'bass-heavy' in comparison with other music of his era. He often composed his great choruses 'from the bass up'.

**'Behold, a Virgin shall conceive –
O thou that tellest'** (alto and chorus)
Behold a Virgin shall conceive and bear a Son,
and shall call his name Emmanuel, God with us.
Isaiah 7:14   *Matthew* 1:23

O thou that tellest good tidings to Zion,
get thee up into the high mountains.
O thou that tellest good tidings to Jerusalem,
lift up thy voice with strength;
lift it up, be not afraid;
say unto the cities of Judah, behold your God!
Isaiah 40:9

Arise, shine, for thy light is come,
and the glory of the Lord is risen upon thee.
Isaiah 60:1

In a short *secco recitative* (without orchestra – literally 'dry' – only the voice with simple harpsichord or continuo accompaniment), the alto predicts the virgin birth of Christ. This is followed by the joyful aria and chorus 'O thou that tellest'. Handel again paints musical pictures as the singer commands the messenger to 'get thee up into the high mountain'. The

The Nativity (right), is the fulfilment of the prophecies made ecstatically by the chorus in the first part of Handel's Messiah *also known as* The Sacred Oratorio: 'Behold a virgin shall conceive and bear a Son, and shall call his name Emmanuel, God with us.'

mountain's height is displayed in a lengthy ornamented passage. The phrase 'Behold your God!' is dramatically set, and quickly followed by another bravura depiction of the light-filled 'Glory of the Lord'. The chorus takes up the strain and again encourages man to 'Behold the glory of the Lord'.

'For unto us a Child is born' (chorus)
For unto us a Child is born, unto us a Son is given,
and the government shall be upon His shoulder;
and His name shall be called Wonderful,
Counsellor, The Mighty God,
The Everlasting Father, The Prince of Peace.
Isaiah 9:5

This chorus started life as an Italian chamber duet written just before *Messiah*. The text is 'No, I don't want to trust myself to you, blind Love, cruel beauty!'

Example 2

No, di voi non vo' fi – dar-mi cie-co A-mor crü-del bel-tà!

Handel reworked it into a jubilant chorus. Some have criticized his scansion of the English text, but this is surely to quibble over genius. If the beginning 'For' is a trifle over-stressed, the wrongly accented 'Wonderful!' perfectly expresses the joyful acclamation of Christ by mankind. Also within this chorus, Handel gives an example of fugal entry for all the parts of the chorus. They enter, first in the tenor then in the soprano and finally in the alto and bass together, in staggered ranks until the exclamations 'Wonderful! Counsellor! The Mighty God!' unite them in a glorious hymn of praise.

**'Then shall the eyes of the Blind –
He shall feed His flock'** (alto, soprano)
Then shall the eyes of the blind be opened,
and the ears of the deaf unstopped.
Then shall the lame man leap as an hart,
and the tongue of the dumb shall sing.
Isaiah 35:5–6

He shall feed his flock like a shepherd;
and He shall gather the lambs with His arm,
and carry them in His bosom,
and gently lead those that are with young.
Isaiah 40:11

Come unto Him, all ye that labour,
ye that are heavy laden, and He will give you rest.
Take His yoke upon you, and learn of Him,
for He is meek and lowly of heart,
and ye shall find rest unto your souls.
Matthew 11:28–29

These short biblical passages describe Christ's wanderings on earth. In a secco recitative, the alto soloist witnesses Christ's miraculous healing of the sick. The alto's following air has a quiet pastoral quality as she likens the Messiah to a shepherd gently tending his flock.

Understanding music: the oratorio and the cantata

Although Handel invented the peculiarly English form of oratorio – exemplified by his *Messiah* – for which he remains justly famous, the form really began more than a century earlier, around 1600, in Italy. In order to get the youth of Rome off its streets, Fillipo Neri, a priest, established a series of musical entertainments in the oratory of Santa Maria church; the theme of each entertainment was of course religious, and there was a sermon in the middle – which explains the essentially sectional structure, as well as the name, of the oratorio form.

Basically an extension of the medieval mystery play, early oratorios included dances, dramatic portrayal and hymn-singing. The Passion story itself, however, was considered too sacred a theme for such treatment. So by 1650, Giacomo Carissimi had written *Jephte*, a short, sombre oratorio with several characters and a narrator, based on a biblical story and rather operatic in style. Handel himself used the story in *Jephtha* 102 years later.

Neither the French nor the Italians developed a tradition of writing oratorios, but the form was adapted in Germany where mainly Gospel texts were used and set to the robust counterpoint of Protestant church music.

It was Handel who perfected the oratorio, creating an almost new form in the process. However, his oratorios were performed by opera singers in a theatre which is still the case today.

In the 19th century, both Beethoven and Schubert unsuccessfully tried their hand at oratorios but it was not until Mendelssohn, with *St Paul* (1836) that the form was reborn.

In 1854 Berlioz wrote *L'enfance du Christ* to his own words and Gounod composed *The Redemption* in 1882. In Britain Elgar wrote *The Dream of Gerontius* using as text a poem by Cardinal Newman, first performed in Birmingham in 1900 while Sir William Walton wrote *Belshazzar's Feast* in 1931.

The cantata

Originally, in the late 1600s and early 1700s, the cantata was a secular (non-religious) form comprising a sequence – recitative-aria-recitative-aria – for solo voice and accompaniment. The cantata soon came to be extended by an initial prelude (or overture) and by the use of more than one soloist when required. First taken up by the Italians, the form influenced Handel in England, and Charpentier and Rameau in France.

But in Germany the chamber cantata became the church cantata, and accordingly incorporated at least one of the already well-known hymns called chorales, either as a movement or as a theme for the whole work. Buxtehude, Bach and Telemann wrote mainly this kind of cantata. The prelude became an opening chorus, and the work generally ended with the chorale; the effect was again essentially theatrical. Since about 1800 the term has been applied to virtually any choral work.

Due to the Bishop of London's ban on stage representations of sacred subjects, Handel's oratorio Esther *was performed in a tavern. The great success of this first oratorio heard in London was followed by the composition of several others, many of whose very popular performances were directed by Handel himself (right).*

Fotomas Index

Titian depicted Christ on the Via Dolorosa as he is helped with his cross by Simon of Cyrene. It is a gesture of kindness contrasted with the cruelty of the crucifixion. In the second part of Messiah *the bass sings: 'the rulers take counsel together against the Lord, and against His Anointed'.*

Titian 'Jesus and the Cyrenian'. Prado, Madrid/Scala

Part The Second

The second section of Handel's Messiah paints a vivid picture of the suffering and torment of the son of God, and mankind's refusal to accept His offer to set them free through the Messiah's Act of Redemption and the over-whelming power of the Lord God Almighty.

'Why do the nations' (bass)
Why do the nations so furiously rage together,
and why do the people imagine a vain thing?
The kings of the earth rise up, and the rulers take
counsel together against the Lord,
and against His Anointed.

Psalms 2:1–2

This bass air is violent, and ornamented with appropriately furious passagework for the strings. The singer also ornaments the word 'rage' to emphasize the futile struggling of 'the kings of the earth' and 'the rulers' who attempt to confound the will of the Lord.

'Thou shalt break them' – (tenor)
Thou shalt break them with a rod of iron;
Thou shalt dash them in pieces
like a potter's vessel.

Psalms 2:9

The tenor aria is accompanied by a leaping figure in the strings which depicts God

swinging His rod of iron down upon His enemies.

'Hallelujah' (chorus)
Hallelujah: for the Lord God Omnipotent
reigneth.

Apocalypse 19:6

The kingdom of this World is become the
kingdom
of our Lord, and of His Christ; and He shall
reign for ever and ever, King of Kings
and Lord of Lords.

Apocalypse 11:15

Hallelujah!

This is the most famous chorus in all classical music, wonderful in its simplicity and boldness of effect. Its festive mood has expressed the joy of man in his Saviour for generations. And the entry of drums and trumpets make the whole shine with excitement. But there is one tradition connected with it which should be quietly put to rest: it is not necessary to stand during the 'Hallelujah Chorus' as if it were a National Anthem. The tradition stems from a performance when the audience were 'so transported that they all together with the king (George II happened to be present) started up and remained standing till the chorus ended'.

Part the Third

'I know that my Redeemer liveth' (soprano)
I know that my Redeemer liveth, and He shall
stand at the latter day upon the earth.
And though worms destoy this body,
yet in my flesh shall I see God.

Job 19:25–25

For now is Christ risen from the dead,
the first-fruits of them that sleep.

1 Corinthians 15:20

This soprano aria is a simple and moving
declaration of faith in the promise of
resurrection. Its intensity, and the clarity
and purity of the setting of the text have
made it a universal favourite.

'The trumpet shall sound' (bass)
The trumpet shall sound, and the
dead shall be raised incorruptible, and
we shall be changed.
For this corruptible must put on incorruption and
this mortal must put on immortality.

1 Corinthians 15:52–53

This bass air has a splendid part for solo
trumpet. The martial atmosphere conjures
up a dramatic vision of the Day of Judge-
ment and the more melodramatic side of
resurrection. The sustained note on the
word 'sound' enables the bass to mimic the
effect of that last trumpet call.

Example 3

The trum-pet shall sound.

'Worthy is the Lamb – Amen' (Chorus)
Worthy is the Lamb that was slain,
and hath redeemed us to God and His blood,
to receive power, and riches, and wisdom, and
strength, and honour, and glory, and blessing.
Blessing and honour, glory and power, be
unto Him that sitteth upon the throne, and
unto the Lamb, for ever and ever.

Apocalypse 5:9, 12–13

Amen.

The magnificent four-square statement of
the final text is followed by an amazing
display of counterpoint as all the voices
interact with a fluidity and flexibility
matched by no other composer. As for the
magnificent virtuoso setting of the final
word 'Amen', the 81 bars of the 'Amen
chorus' demonstrate Handel's remarkable
contrapuntal skill and exemplifies the
genius of whom the poet Cowper wrote:

*Remember Handel? Who, that was not
born Deaf as the dead to harmony,
forgets,
Or can, the more than Homer of his age?*

**The soprano rejoices 'For now is Christ
risen from the dead', in the third section
of Messiah. The Ascension of Christ is here
depicted by Rembrandt, a painter
Handel greatly admired.**

Great interpreters

Soloists

Heather Harper

The soprano Heather Harper was born in Belfast in 1930 and studied music at Trinity College. In 1955, while a member of the chorus at Glyndebourne, she was hired for a BBC production of *La Traviata,* singing the lead. This gave her the national exposure she needed, and the acclaim that greeted her performance led to successful roles with every major British operatic company within the next few years. At the same time she became quickly established as a popular concert singer, and her performances in oratorio and concert works have led to many triumphs.

Since the early 1960s her reputation has been world-wide and she has toured Europe on many occasions, as well as the USA and Australia. Her range of roles and musical scope are remarkably diverse while her fine singing of Benjamin Britten's music, both in opera and song, is undoubtedly a highlight, as is her work in oratorios such as Handel's *Messiah.*

Helen Watts

Helen Watts was born in Milford Haven in 1927. After initial indecision as to her vocation, she studied at the Royal Academy of Music, then proceeded to voice training under a succession of teachers. She soon developed her natural contralto into a strong and versatile voice. Her professional career began with the BBC Chorus, though before long she advanced to the lead role in a broadcast of Gluck's *Orpheus and Eurydice.* Her career rapidly accelerated after the success of this début, and by the late 1950s she was regarded as one of the leading singers of oratorio in the country. By the mid 1960s her talent was recognized world-wide, though she herself was not content to remain just within oratorios. Early successes with operas by Handel were followed by subsequent roles in both Britten and Wagner productions. At the same time she continued diversifying into music such as Schoenberg and Brahms. She now has a command of virtually every type of classical contralto singing.

John Shirley-Quirk

Born in Liverpool in 1931, baritone Shirley-Quirk has for long been conspicuous on the British music scene. After initially making chemistry his career at Liverpool University, he abandoned this vocation and went to London in 1961 to study singing with Roy Henderson. He sang in St Paul's Cathedral Choir for the following two years before appearing at Glyndebourne for the first time, where he was well received. Since then he has reappeared at Glyndebourne many times in such operas as *Pelleas et Melisande* and *Capriccio.*

As a solo singer he has made many

John Shirley-Quirk (far left) and Heather Harper (left), two highly respected soloists whose interpretation of Messiah has brought them acclaim throughout the world.

concert appearances and recordings, excelling particularly in British song. As an opera singer he has been closely associated with a number of Britten's operas. He is a first-rate oratorio singer, both modern and classical, as his interpretations of both Delius and Handel demonstrate. His richness of voice and sensitivity to the work at hand have made him in constant demand all over the world.

Performing Messiah

The history of *Messiah* is the history of an enormous variety of performing circumstances. Even in Handel's own day the size of the choir and orchestra was often adapted by the composer to fit individual circumstances. During the last century it became customary to give performances of the work with colossally inflated numbers of singers and players, which made it totally out of keeping with Handel's intentions.

In more modern times this overly-pompous approach to the work has been gradually discarded as increasing numbers of performers and listeners have become interested in establishing what Handel himself has written and called for. Recent performances reflect that trend. For a start, the orchestral numbers are few, and the instruments used are the ones to be found in Handel's own score. There are 31 strings, two oboes, two bassoons, two trumpets, timpani, Baroque chamber organ, and harpsichord. There are 40 voices in the chorus.

Conductors and singers have also been at pains to present the work as a cohesive whole, rather than a series of brilliant and oppressive flights of musical or vocal vituosity. In this they feel they are adhering to the spirit of the composer's own wishes for the music.

Music for the Royal Fireworks and Water Music

The contrasting moods of a party on the river and a national celebration of peace gave Handel the chance to show his brilliance at composing for great occasions outdoors.

The Music for the Royal Fireworks and the Water Music, pieces commissioned by two Hanoverian kings, show Handel's supreme skill in composing outdoor occasional music. When Handel wrote for George I, in the early 1700s, his star was already in the ascendant and, by the time he came to write the Music for the Royal Fireworks for George II, he was firmly established as the 'composer-laureate' of Britain.

Before they were published, both pieces were arranged for a conventional 'indoor' orchestra – thankfully, without spoiling their open-air feel. This was partly because they made use of standard Baroque devices such as hunting call refrains echoed by brass or by imitative figures in the woodwinds or strings. The Baroque delight in balancing small groups of solo instruments (concertino) against other sections of the whole orchestra (tutti) is also evident. In addition, Handel's personal love of complex counterpoint and rich harmonies had been directed towards creating a clear texture for the brass parts. This careful composition prevents the muddy tones that might have resulted from the peculiar acoustics of playing in the open air. Together, therefore, these two pieces represent a peak in the composition of outdoor music and have become the most popular orchestral works ever composed by Handel.

Music for the Royal Fireworks

The Peace of Aix-la-Chapelle, which ended the War of the Austrian Succession, was formally signed in 1748. George II hoped and expected that a burst of enthusiastic publicity would surround what he saw as one of the great triumphs of his reign. The war had dragged on for eight indecisive years and George had been so committed to its success that he had personally led his troops into the field in 1743 (the last king of England to do this). Although critics later made disparaging remarks about the 'ageing little king', he and his men did win a notable victory on the day. When he returned to London, the crowds welcomed him triumphantly, but the war dragged on. Five years later, both king and country were heartily glad to see the conflict finally resolved and George II was not above exploiting its limited propaganda value.

Plans for the festivities were begun well in advance, a brilliant fireworks display decided on and Handel was chosen to compose a great outdoor concerto to introduce the pyrotechnics. By now, Handel was the 'grand old man' of English music. Like George II, he was probably also a little set in his ways. As a result, the organization of the great display caused considerable problems. The letters written by the Duke of Montague, Master General of the Ordnance, to Charles Frederick, 'Comptroller of His Majesty's Fireworks as well as for War as for Triumph', give a delightful peep at the behind-the-scenes preparations – and headaches! Montague's fretting about 'Hendel' (Handel) and the King is especially revealing.

I think Hendel now proposes to have but 12 trumpets and 12 French horns; at first there was to have been sixteen of each, and I remember I told the King so, who, at that time, objected to there being any musick; but when I told him the quantity and nomber of martial musick there was to be, he was better satisfied, and said he hoped there would be no fiddles. Now Hendel proposes to lessen the nomber of trumpets, etc. and to have violeens. I dont at all doubt but when the King hears it he will be very much displeased.

To make matters worse for poor Montague, a huge architectural backdrop had been commissioned from Giovanni Niccolo Servandoni, an architect who

specialized in theatrical scenery. It must have been a tense time, too, for Charles Frederick, the 'Comptroller'; even the rehearsal was a calendar event, with an orchestra of over 100 pieces and an audience of 12,000. It caused one of the first ever recorded traffic jams in London!

So great a resort occasioned such a stoppage on LONDON BRIDGE that no carriage could pass for 3 hours. The footmen were so numerous as to obstruct the passage, so that a scuffle happen'd, in which some gentlemen were wounded.

Finally the day of the performance arrived. Handel's music was played by a huge band placed under the central arch of the structure. Then the fireworks began. The original idea was of a Baroque 'son et lumière' on the subject of Peace, but things did not go quite as planned. Unfortunately, Servandoni's structure caught fire!

While the pavillion was on fire, the Chevalier SERVANDONI, who designed the building, drawing his sword and affronting Charles Frederick Esq., Comptroller of the Ordnance and Fireworks, he was disarmed and taken into custody, but discharg'd the next day on asking pardon before the Duke of Cumberland.

At least Handel's music was a success!

In 1748 the Peace of Aix-la-Chapelle was signed – one of the personal triumphs of George II's reign. He himself had led his troops into battle (below right) and was quick to exploit the propaganda value of this victory. Public festivities in celebration of the peace were on a lavish scale. One of the highlights was a spectacular firework display along continental lines (right and below left) which united the genius of a great British composer, Handel (albeit born in Germany), with an inspired French stage designer, Servandoni (albeit sporting a most Italianate name)!

Programme notes

Handel's scoring for the Music for the Royal Fireworks consists of 24 oboes, 12 bassoons, 1 contra-bassoon, 9 trumpets; 9 horns and 3 pairs of timpani. Even by adding side-drums (to bring the drums up to an equal 9), there is a large gap in the number of players if it was meant to total 100. It would appear, therefore, that despite Montague's fretting, and the King's hostility, Handel kept his 'violeens'. Certainly, he included strings in the later performances he directed.

The Fireworks music itself is, in fact, a grand suite of what was known as 'character symphonies'. Following the French style, the *Ouverture* combines a slow, expansive opening, marked by dotted rhythms and suspensions, with a lively, fugal-type allegro. The grandeur of the introduction is stated in solemn, sustained notes that make use of the entire orchestra and startle the listener to attention.

Example 1

From this beginning, it divides into a series of calls and answers between the various sections of the band. The driving rhythm concentrates on military brilliance, like Baroque open-air music for equestrian displays or military exercises. It was also a style that was extremely popular in the court of Louis XV, and has a courtly grace and elegance despite its bright pace. Handel's version gradually increases the complexity of musical textures as trumpets, oboes and ringing horns overlap with one another in festive celebration.

The opening mood changes noticeably as a lively *Bourrée* breaks into its stride, providing light relief amid the military mood of the surrounding movements. The oboes take up their sprightly display with bright enthusiasm and the jovial tone of a French folk dance is happily sustained throughout.

La Paix, a flowing, atmospheric piece is the symbolic centre of the suite, bearing as it does the title 'Peace'. The solemn mood of the oboes is repeated by the horns to create an evocative image of pastoral peace and calm.

Example 2

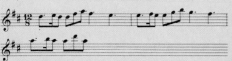

Outdoor fêtes were all the rage among Europe's nobility (above), and on the day of the firework display Green Park was decked out for a right royal occasion. Handel's music perfectly reflected the open-air atmosphere – but unfortunately not everything went to plan. The highlight of the entertainment for some was when Servandoni's magnificent pavillion caught fire (left)!

After 'Peace' comes *La Réjouissance,* the rejoicing. This is a boisterous allegro, played by trumpets, woodwind and strings with answering cheers from the horns and woodwind section. The side drums add to the texture and, for the first time, seem to anticipate the impending noise and colour of the fireworks display. Finally, all the players jubilantly thunder out the theme together.

The *Menuet and Trio* that follows is a rather stately affair, with prominent side drums to emphasize the military under-tones of the whole suite. The minuet is interrupted by an alternative theme played first by the woodwind and then by the strings. A triumphant restatement of the first melody by all the orchestra, brimming over with confidence, brings the suite to a joyful and extrovert conclusion before the fireworks begin. There is nothing to suggest, however, that the music was played during the display itself.

Understanding music: occasional music

Today, musical performances tend to be confined to certain particular times and places – largely concert halls and opera houses – and are usually given for paying audiences. But in earlier centuries music played a very different role in that it was not available to all on a regular basis. Musicians, particularly composers, were generally retained by wealthy patrons and their duty was to provide music to order, as and when the patron wanted. Frequently, music would be requested in celebration of a special event and given its premiere at the 'occasion'. Such music, therefore, assumed particular importance by being an integral part of occasions and because it was heard by a larger and wider audience than usual.

As early as the 15th century at Con-stantinople, music played a central part in the festivities surrounding the gather-ing of Europe's nobles at the 'Feast of the Pheasant' – given to promote a cru-sade. Later, in 1589 the celebratory music composed for another great occa-sion – the wedding of Duke Ferdinand de' Medici and Christine of Lorraine – had a great impact on future musical development. At that time plays were often performed as a normal part of festivities and the acts were separated by short, contrasting tableaux, called *intermedii,* which often incorporated music and dancing. At these wedding celebrations, the intermedii were so lavish that they completely over-shadowed the plays themselves – and it was from such intermedii that opera as we know it today developed.

When Charles II was restored to the English throne in 1660, he set up a substantial musical establishment and he was also served by some very fine composers, including Henry Purcell. Among the many occasional works which Purcell wrote for Charles and his successors were several 'Odes' in celebration of the Queen's birthday or St Cecilia's Day, and the magnificent, sombre Funeral Music for Queen Mary. Another particularly fertile area of ceremonial composition was, of course, the coronation anthem: Handel's *Zadok the Priest* written for the coronation of George II, has since been sung at the coronation of every successive English monarch – including George IV (right).

A constantly recurring aspect of occasional music was its 'outdoor' element. Mozart wrote many serenades for outdoor performance while in the service of the Archbishop of Salzburg: the larger ones were designed for grand celebrations like the Archbishop's name-day, or society weddings – the hour-long 'Haffner' Serenade was written for the wedding of the daughter of the Burgomaster of Salzburg – while the lesser *divertimenti* were intended for smaller, family occasions. These are usually scored for several pairs of wind instrument.

In 1840, the French government com-missioned Berlioz to compose a work for the inauguration of the Column of the Bastille. The resulting *Symphonie Funèbre et Triomphale* was scored for a huge military band of 207 instruments, 33 of which were clarinets!

There are still many musical works written to celebrate particular occasions, but their performance is more usually confined indoors. When Brahms was awarded an honorary degree from the University of Breslau in 1879, the university expected a new composition in return; two years later, Brahms himself conducted in a special concert the first performance of his 'Academic Festival' Overture, in which university life is celebrated by the inclusion of several popular student songs.

Today, the occasions commemorated in music are many and varied. The 'Severn Bridge' Variations, written to celebrate that bridge's completion, includes movements by seven com-posers, including Michael Tippett and Malcolm Arnold. Recently, of course, there was in Britain a return to the grand, royal, musical occasion with the wedding of the Prince of Wales, when the wedding anthem was, appropriately, commissioned from a leading Welsh composer, William Mathias. But even on that occasion, Handel had the last word, with his splendidly virtuosic aria, *Let the bright seraphim.*

Water Music

Much of what we now know as the Water Music was probably composed or arranged for an evening concert on the River Thames in July, 1717, although some pieces had been composed before that time. It is still possible to find written versions of a popular myth concerning the origins of this piece – a hoary tale which first appeared in the Handel biography published in 1760.

According to the tale, Handel was in disgrace with his former employer, the Elector of Hanover, because he had overstayed his 'leave of absence' at the court of Queen Anne. When the Queen died, her heir was the Elector – George I. The king apparently carried his hostility towards Handel across the channel and would have remained disenchanted with him but for the timely intervention of a certain Baron Kielmansegg. The baron arranged for a rapprochement between the king and his errant 'capellmeister' by means of the delightful music Handel composed for a royal river party. In all, it seems a plausible tale, but sadly it is incorrect in almost every detail♦

The idea for a river outing actually came from the king himself and was to be like the masquerades (by Heidegger) that he enjoyed watching at the Haymarket Theatre. Baron Kielmansegg paid for the extravaganza and, according to a report sent to the Prussian court, the entire outing proved extremely successful:

The music was composed especially by the celebrated Handel, a native of Halle, and His Majesty's principal Court Composer. His Majesty approved of it so greatly that he caused it to be repeated three times in all, although each performance lasted an hour – namely twice before and once after supper. The evening was all that could be desired for the festivity, the number of barges and above all of boats desirous of hearing was beyond counting.

No autograph score has yet been found for the Water Music, although several manuscripts have come to light. A set of instrumental parts for a chamber suite which pre-dates the Water Music publication has been identified and contemporary newspaper advertisements for Handel performances indicate much lost music that he probably used to compile the orchestral version in use today.

Programme notes

Water Music Suite in D

The music in the D major suite is scored for trumpets and horns as well as oboes, bassoons, strings and continuo and is very much in the French style.

The *Prelude,* with its clear, ringing tones, is festive and march-like, making a

Archiv für Kunst und Geschichte

Handel's delightful Water Music (the first page of one of several existing manuscripts is shown right) was prepared for a concert on the River Thames in July 1717. George I himself had the happy idea of a river party and, when the day arrived, Handel joined the King in the royal barge (above), while the musicians sailed alongside.

showpiece for trumpets and answering horns (French horns were an innovation in orchestral writing at that time: Handel was to cause a sensation by using them in his opera *Radamisto,* in 1719). The repeated calls on the trumpets and horn responses

Example 3
Alia hornpipe

Fitzwilliam Museum

Progressing from one dance form to another, *Lentement* (Slowly), has a swaying, rocking motion that is full of happy good humour. Woodwind and strings set the mood, but once again the irrepressible trumpets open and close the melody.

In the *Bourrée,* a dance is once more transformed into a vehicle for brass exchanges. After the relatively quiet and sedate dances beforehand, we suddenly return to the brightly contrasting calls of trumpets and horns. The mood and rhythm shifts magically away from scenes of courtly elegance and the conclusion is one of lively celebration.

Water Music Suite in F

The outstanding characteristic of the F major suite is its striking horn passages, which must have resounded across the Thames with breathtaking magnificence. It consists of ten numbers scored for oboes, bassoons, horns, strings and continuo.

The suite opens with a very grand *Ouverture* in the French style (a dignified slow movement followed by a fast second section). Handel's introductory section is suitably sedate but a brisk fugal section follows, with a concertino of two violins and oboe chattering away above the more serious musical debate of the strings.

The solemn mood is carried through into the *Adagio e staccato* – a slow, recitative passage with a plaintive solo and string accompaniment which gives the oboist a chance for a quiet, contemplative display tinged with melancholy.

Suddenly the mood is turned upside down and a brisk *Hornpipe* (allegro) raises the tempo. Since the hornpipe was a sailors' dance, its appearance at a boating party was singularly appropriate, but Handel once again lifts the traditional form and turns it into a jubilant song for the orchestra.

One of the novelties of the Water Music Suites is the prominent role played by the French Horn; (the title page to Walsh's Forest Harmony, *which published several 'Curious Pieces' from the Water Music, makes great play of this fact, below). With its repertoire of hunting calls (above right) and hornpipes, the instrument was ideally suited to the open air.*

Example 4

culminate in a wonderfully bold 'brass duet'. These resonant fanfares then give way to recitative-like passage for the strings, whose swaying melody is in slower, more lyrical tempo.

The *Hornpipe* is one of the most famous pieces in the entire collection. Handel based his music on the traditional sailors' dance, but the echoing effects of trumpets, answered by horns, transform it into an exuberant musical exchange which conjures up vivid images of the hunt as well as of the high seas.

The fanfare motifs not only balance against each other but are also interrupted by sweeping passages for strings and woodwind. In brilliant style, however, it is the resounding brass which has the last word in these contrasting sections.

The *Minuet,* which follows immediately after this lively hornpipe, provides a serene pause full of elegant little flourishes. Again, the movement gives voice to the trumpets and horns, but here they respect the quiet dignity of a stately court dance.

The woodwind repeat this lively figure, with light-hearted trills on the final horn notes and an overall effect of sustained brilliance.

The *Andante* which follows is a stately, contrasting piece for oboes, bassoon and strings in D minor. The self-assurance of this gentle processional music provides a moment of calm in the series of joyously extrovert dances. An oboe solo leads into the allegro repeat, then gives way to the harder tones of two horns. The final page joins the entire orchestra in a delightful great downhill dash.

In the *Jig,* a *passpied* or fast minuet, the

St James' Park (left) – seen here from the terrace of no. 10 Downing St – was the final destination of the royal barging party. They arrived here in high spirits – at half past four in the morning.

Canaletto's painting of a royal river outing on the Thames (below) richly evokes the original setting of Handel's Water Music. The endless variety of boats and barges must have made this a truly memorable occasion.

horns are prominent. Their calls are echoed by strings and oboes and bassoon but the texture is nonetheless considerably more reserved than the preceding hornpipe. The opening horns step aside for a long, gentle passage for strings and then, at the end, they quietly tiptoe back, as if reluctant to break the mood.

This sense of quiet and calm continues in the *Air* – a soft, lilting dance movement whose sighing, melancholy melody is decorated by sustained notes in the horns, suspended behind the lyrical string texture.

Example 5

This gives a curious 'floating' effect and the lengthened horn calls must have carried wonderfully along the Thames as the royal party drifted contentedly on their way.

The world of courtly dignity returns in Handel's lovely *Minuet*. A central section features the bassoon, but the opening and closing horn entries mingle hunting calls with the restraint of the triple rhythm. This is, in fact, the last appearance of the horns in the entire suite.

A fussy little *Bourrée* for bassoons, oboes and strings follows the minuet with an insistent, rhythmic drive. The bourrée was a lively French dance which would have kept the courtiers on their toes – certainly its energetic rhythm appealed to many Baroque composers. Handel, however, creates a wonderfully comic effect, and his version bustles along with breathtaking speed and delicacy!

The bourrée is immediately followed by a *Hornpipe* which is scored for the same

instruments and with equal gentility. The sailor dancing this must have been to finishing school! Nevertheless the precise, angular phrasing and pure tones retain an authentic, folk-like quality.

The final movement, a *Gavotte* in D minor (scored for two oboes, bassoon and strings) does not fit comfortably with the suites and may have been intended as an alternative for the Andante passage. It is, however, a superb composition and well worth inclusion. It has repeated figures with an oboe solo that resounds like an unanswered question and lingers plaintively at the end.

It is scarcely surprising that the King and his party enjoyed the music so whole-heartedly. Their evening was rounded off by a 'choice supper' in Chelsea and the King returned home in the early hours of the morning. The concert cost Baron Kielmansegg £150 for the musicians alone – surely a worthwhile investment!

Great interpreters

The Academy

The Academy of St Martin-in-the-Fields was founded in 1957 when a group of players, organized by Neville Marriner, began a series of chamber recitals at the famous church (St Martin's) in Charing Cross, London. It was conceived as a small ensemble, recruited on individual merit from all the best orchestras in London, who could meet together for occasional recitals. After making their first record in 1959, they met with great critical and popular success. Since that time, the group has continued to come together for about three months a year to give recitals or fulfil recording schedules as they choose. Neville Marriner still holds the post of director.

Neville Marriner (director)

Marriner, who was born in London in 1924, was taught the violin by his father. After further private coaching, he entered the Royal College of Music in 1937 but his studies were interrupted by service in the army during World War II. After the war, he completed his studies in London before moving on to further training at the Paris Conservatoire.

His return to England brought him into contact with an old friend, Thurston Dart, and together they formed a duo specializing in 17th and 18th century music. In 1948, Marriner was appointed professor at the Royal College, though he continued performing. By 1950, he and Dart, under the guise of the Jacobean Ensemble, made their first records (Purcell's Trio Sonatas, for Argo) and they continued to make chamber recordings for much of the 1950s. In 1956, Marriner joined the London Symphony Orchestra as principal second violin, remaining until 1969.

The event which was to lead to his developing an international reputation as a conductor however, was the formation of the Academy in 1957. Marriner had been invited by the director of music at St Martin's to form a performing ensemble for music after evensong. The success of this group led to appearances on record for L'Oiseau Lyre and Argo, a great many of which were critically acclaimed for their professional expertise and their accurate playing of pre-Romantic music. After a study visit to the USA in 1959, where he was trained on the finer points of conducting by Pierre Monteux, Marriner led the Academy with a new sense of purpose and decisiveness. Because of this, and the long series of recordings undertaken for Argo, the group's fame spread throughout the world.

In 1969, Marriner accepted an invitation to direct the then newly-formed Los Angeles Chamber Orchestra and, each year since, he has spent three months conducting them in a broad repertoire of music. His success has led to a host of invitations to conduct major US orchestras.

Marriner does not see it as the Academy's place to use original instruments for their performances, even though they have done so much to stimulate interest in the music of the 17th and 18th centuries. He and the Academy prefer to be an ensemble that plays music from all periods, knowing there will always be appreciation for a performance which exhibits fidelity of interpretation and brilliant execution on modern instruments.

The ensemble playing elicited by Marriner is clean, crisp and incisive and his conducting style seeks bright, clear tones and a transparency of texture that reveals the pieces' true colours.

FURTHER LISTENING

Handel concertos and vocal music

Organ Concerti op. 4

Handel was always an unorthodox composer, intent on practical and imaginative solutions to musical and professional challenges. In practice this led him to make some historic innovations – he wrote the first organ concertos and introduced the English oratorio to the world. That in itself might not have been sufficient claim to immortality, but Handel's concertos, although a disparate collection originally played in intervals between sections of his oratorios, are of great worth and considerable charm. Handel revelled in the chance to display the soloist's virtuosity against the orchestral background and the range of mood and texture in these six concertos alone makes for rewarding listening.

Concerti Grossi op. 6

By the time this second collection of orchestral concertos was published (1739), Handel was long used to giving his public just what they wanted. As a result, these works are written with popular Italianate models in mind, though they contain much of the quirkiness, unpredictability of structure and line, and sheer musical personality which has endeared Handel to generations of music-lovers. His subtlety and craft is evident in all 12 concertos.

Ode for St Cecilia's Day

In setting Dryden's ode to music, Handel looked to the composer Purcell for some of his inspiration. The Ode is a delightful short work in which both the arias and choruses show consistently fine, beguiling and beautiful musical thought.

In the background

Scientists still argue whether our natures or our upbringing contribute most to our personalities, talents and behaviour. However, it is undeniable that we cannot help being affected to some extent by our surroundings. Great composers are no exception, and the following pages describe the historical background to Handel's life, and the events that influenced and inspired him: the city of London that he knew and made his home; and the revolution in scientific thought that changed forever the way in which humanity views the world. Seen against the stultifying reputation of its kings (and Handel's patrons), George I and George II, and the dominating presence of Sir Robert Walpole, mid-18th century England can seem placid to the point of tedium. But it was a time of almost continuous war (the Music for the Royal Fireworks originally celebrated the Treaty of Aix-la-Chapelle), and was a period of great cultural vigour amongst whose products Handel's music stands as a notable example.

IN THE BACKGROUND

Handel's London

That great sage, Dr Samuel Johnson, once declared that 'when a man is tired of London, he is tired of life; for there is in London all that life can afford', while just over a hundred years later, Conan Doyle in A Study in Scarlet described the city as 'that great cesspool'. The two descriptions are not, of course, mutually exclusive, and as we know from the novels of Defoe, Richardson and Fielding, 18th-century London, or 'the great wen' was a city of immense contrasts. The absence of an effective police force and the general availability of weapons made the crime rate very high, while the low price of alcohol meant that drunkenness was a severe problem. At the same time, London was a centre of culture. The actor David Garrick was at the height of his powers, and Handel's operas were being given their first performances, while in the coffee houses Johnson, whose conversations Boswell so vividly reported, held the company spellbound.

IN THE BACKGROUND
'The great wen'

A city and a society of extreme contrasts, Handel's London was the metropolis of Dr Johnson and his circle, of coffee-houses and pleasure gardens, and of a buoyant commercial life.

By the 1750s London was already a great city, a 'metropolis' as it was then usually called. No longer just an overgrown town, it boasted fine houses and streets and squares in classical style, which made it an elegant place in which to live and to visit.

London consisted of the City proper and what is now central London. In the 18th century the City (as now) stretched from Temple Bar in the Strand to the Tower. Those who lived there were the poor and the tradesman-class, known as the 'Cits'. High society had already moved out of the City and lived west of Temple Bar – beginning to form what we now know as the West End. Temple Bar itself, an imposing edifice which inconveniently narrowed the street, was regularly the scene of one example of the age's morbid streak: until 1776 the smart could hire spy-glasses to view the rotting heads of traitors that had been stuck on top since the 1745 Jacobite rebellion.

The 'West End' occupied only a few square miles, with part of the lived-in district dribbling along the Thames down to Westminster. Here, the House of Commons was not the relatively orderly place we know today. Many booted and spurred members in greatcoats could be seen stretched out asleep on the benches, or eating oranges and cracking nuts, while a debate was in progress.

Although many of the houses of London were grand, the streets were often filthy. They did, however, teem with life: strollers and people on

One of the most 'colourful' spots of 18th-century London was Covent Garden (below). Its busy vegetable market was one of the specialist markets used by 18th-century Londoners. And the piazza itself offered much in the way of entertainment – tea- and coffee-houses and bawdy taverns.

The kings whose reigns spanned Handel's career in London: George I (far left) became king in 1717 even though he couldn't speak the language – something which prompted the development of cabinet government. Although his son, George II (left), did speak English, he was an equally 'stupid but complicated' person. He was succeeded by his grandson, George III (right) his son, Frederick, having died from a chill caught while playing tennis.

Visually, Georgian London was the height of elegance. But the fine clothes, splendid architecture and serene landscapes (above), for which this period is renowned, were only part of a larger, and far less rosy picture. The streets of London were filthy and dangerous (below) and the people seemed cruel and rowdy.

business; sedan-chairs and carriages. Street-traders' cries vied with the noise of iron-rimmed wheels on the cobbles. Although sedan-chairs made no noise the chairmen were often loud, rude and rough – deliberately pushing their poles into passers-by and splashing them with dirt.

Practically policeless and, at night, poorly lit, London had an incredibly high crime-rate – and relatively few criminals were brought to justice. Even in daylight people of all classes were threatened, robbed, beaten-up and murdered. Apart from countless humble citizens, victims of thuggery included the Prince of Wales, the Prime Minister and the Lord Mayor. At night, bells were rung so that revellers from Piccadilly could assemble to be safely escorted back to Kensington Village and foot guards were employed to see people home from the pleasure gardens at Vauxhall and Ranelagh. But the public generally relied only on watchmen, constables and a few Bow Street runners, the forerunners of policemen. But danger lurked even when precautions were taken – the link-boys who lit customers home by torchlight were often in league with robbers.

The first Georges

Georgian London was a city relatively free from the turbulence of the 17th century and the social and intellectual ferment of the 19th. Its apparent stability and prosperous complacency were revealed in politics, religion, commerce, letters, and in the lifestyle of the first Hanoverian kings. The reigns of both George I (1714–27) and George II (1727–60) exhibited an external, though superficial, calmness that rested on the settlement of old quarrels at home and expanding power (naval and commercial) overseas.

George I knew no English when he came to the throne at the age of 54. He acceded by virtue of the Act of Settlement of 1701, which had been passed to prevent a return of the Stuart line, and which had made his mother Sophia, the Electress of Hanover in

Germany, the heir to Queen Anne's throne. But George I had ruled as an autocrat in Hanover and he had little interest in the English people. He was not partial to their liberal consititution and so he left the day-to-day running of affairs to his ministers, most notably Sir Robert Walpole. Like his father, George II was also more interested in Hanover than England and at Dettingen in 1743 he was the last English monarch to lead his army into battle in Europe. Both George I and George II spent much of their reigns out of England, so that the House of Hanover did not become fully naturalized until the reign of George III (1760–1820), who did think of himself as English and who declared that he 'gloried in the name of Briton [sic]'.

Despite the fact that the first two Georges were dull and often boorish kings, the royal court at St James's Palace remained an important social and political centre. Because he had divorced and shut away his queen, George I had no consort to grace his court (though he did have several mistresses). The Prince of Wales, later George II, had a stormy relationship with his father, which may have been partly due to his resentment of the way in which his mother had been treated, but the tension between the king and his heir had a positive social effect.

It meant that the Prince and Princess of Wales's household became a stimulating rival to the actual court, attracting younger, livelier and more ambitious people. The Princess of Wales, Caroline of Anspach, was, moreover, a formidable woman who loved company and gossip, and an infinitely more cultivated personality than George I. But that was not saying very much, for the only art that interested Caroline and George II was music. Indeed, music was George's one delight and he had a passionate interest in opera. It is due as much to George II as anyone that Handel secured the encouragement which led him to settle in England.

George III was another dull king and since he

With gin at a penny a pint, alcoholism was rife among London's poor – though for many a welcome distraction from the rigours of life. Hogarth's 'Gin Lane' (left) pulls no punches in its warning of the ravages of drink. 'Gin cursed Fiend, with Fury fraught Makes human Race a Prey . . .' starts the inscription underneath the print.

Dr Johnson (right), the famous conversationalist and leading light of London society, was a frequent visitor to tea- and coffee-houses (bottom right). These all-male establishments were popular throughout the 18th century.

By Courtesy of the National Portrait Gallery

National Portrait Gallery

Robert Walpole (above), who was Prime Minister from 1721 to 1741, led an efficient but corrupt administration. The 18th-century parliamentary scene was generally riddled with intrigue, rowdiness, and the worst excesses of careerist politics. In Hogarth's 'Election Entertainment' (left) the voters are being fêted by a candidate.

acceded to the throne before he had an heir, restless socialites did not have the compensation of a rival junior royal household. George III was home-loving, parsimonious and morally very correct, and so too was his queen, Charlotte. Even her very first party, given in 1761, was a meagre affair which set the tone for a long reign.

Manners and morals

An invitation to a 'rout' (party), a ball or an assembly in one of London's great houses was far more important to society than one to the fuddy-duddy palace. In these houses people could expect a good time, mingling with celebrities of one kind or another. And here they found what 18th-century society admired most: wealth, wit, taste, cynicism, humour and style.

But high society did not necessarily mean polite society in Handel's London, for a relatively coarse attitude to life and gross manners were general. The language of even the most illustrious citizens, both men and women, was as uninhibited as it was unrefined. Dukes thought nothing of becoming disgustingly drunk in public and fashionable young men – 'rakes', 'Bloods' and 'Nerves' – were particularly addicted to rowdy behaviour in private and in public.

And it was the young men who often attracted the most attention as trendsetters in fashion. They were conspicuous on account of their beautiful manners as well as their outrageous clothes, and they were a gift to caricaturists. Many such dandies may have had homosexual preferences, a 'vice' that was more openly prevalent in the 18th century than most people realize.

However, the extent of this 'vice' was nothing compared with the extent of female prostitution in 18th-century London. High-class courtesans charged as much as 500 guineas for a night. Less well-off men could afford the very cheap attentions of countless girls and women, especially in Covent Garden where there were plenty of brothels and available women in taverns. Green Park at night was a notorious open-air brothel. The authorities locked the gates at dusk but since at least 6,500 people had keys this hardly mattered.

Clubs and coffee houses

For indoor socializing of another kind, there were the gentlemen's clubs, most of which were born in the 18th century, as well as establishments for those functions down the social scale. Men of rank and

Fotomas Index

position met, ate, talked, gambled and relaxed in elegant new premises in St James's or in Pall Mall. Many lesser clubs were held in a room in a tavern. Intellectuals went to debating clubs and the anti-religious joined the notorious 'Hell-Fire' club. More favoured in lower-circles were the 'cock and hen' clubs, the haunts of tarts and villains.

Almac's (later Brooks) was renowned for its excessive gambling, which was in fact a virulent disease all over London. Anything and everything were grounds for a bet and for the rich the stakes were very high. The statesman and orator, Charles Fox, would lose £500 an hour at the gaming tables, while even a poor man would cast away his week's meagre wages at the throw of a dice. The government sponsored state lotteries while a favourite

game in private houses was gold- or silver-loo.

Excessive drinking was another problem in a city where gin was as cheap as a penny a pint and signs outside gin-shops offered an opportunity to get drunk for twopence. Among the poorer citizens, men and women alike, the ravages of alcoholism were most vividly exposed in Hogarth's prints *Gin Lane* and *Beer Street*. Although these savage indictments of the original 'mother's ruin' were executed in the 1750s when government action against cheap drink had commenced, the same state of affairs persisted until the end of the century. Among the upper classes 'two-bottle' men were famous; port was also a very popular drink. In addition to alcohol, Handel's London was also awash with new stimulants as tea, coffee and chocolate

On summer evenings, a favourite pastime for Londoners was a visit to a pleasure garden. The most popular was at Vauxhall (left, illustrating this title page) where people wandered in the spacious grounds and listened to music provided by an orchestra. There were many other forms of entertainment, too, not the least of which was the possibility of a romantic rendezvous.

Although enjoying the genteel side of life, people were, on the whole, very insensitive to the plight of others. Society women, for instance, considered a visit to the lunatics at Bedlam (below) an amusing outing.

One of the plays
enjoyed by the fickle
London theatre-goers
of the 18th century was
John Gay's Beggar's
Opera (left). Audience
participation, as often
as not, involved
hurling abuse – or
indeed whatever was
at hand – at the actors.
But for the most part, as
Hogarth has
caricatured (below),
the audience was
usually more
interested in flirting.

became popular beverages at home as well as in the coffee-houses.

'My face is very well known at the Grecian' wrote James Addison, the essayist and poet, in 1711. He was referring to a coffee-house, the first of which opened in London in 1652. Queen Anne's reign (1702–14) saw the houses' heyday but they were popular throughout the 18th century. Less élitist than the gentlemen's clubs, they were haunts where men could drink coffee and tea, talk politics and indulge in gossip; smoke, play cards and read newspapers.

The pleasure gardens

One of the 18th century's most delightful innovations was the pleasure garden. Including spas, and taverns with bowling-greens, Georgian Londoners had about 50 such 'gardens' – from Hampstead in the north to St Helen's in the south – to choose from. The most fashionable were Vauxhall and Ranelagh, neither of them in what was then London 'proper'. Vauxhall was in the village of Lambeth and Ranelagh just south of what is now Vauxhall Bridge. Both included tree-lined walks (at night, hung with coloured lights), arbours, grottoes, pavilions and refreshment rooms. Ranelagh, the more sophisticated garden, boasted a magnificent Rotunda where people could promenade, listen to music, eat and drink. At Vauxhall there were

fancy-dress balls, and dancing often went on all night. The spa at Sadlers Wells (the theatre was built in 1765) catered for 'lower-class lasses, sailors and other young people dancing'. They were also entertained by pantomines and women wire-walkers.

London's parks have always been the envy of other capitals. Charles I had opened Hyde Park to the public in 1637 and a century later George II added Rotton Row (corrupt pronunciation of *route du roi*), where the fashionable could ride. Green Park was also open to all ranks. Cricket, which was first organized on a county basis in the 18th century, was played at White Conduit Fields in Islington and bare-fist boxing could be enjoyed at Mr Stoke's Amphitheatre in the Islington Road. There were cock-fights at the 'Royal Cock-Pit' in Birdcage Walk, which was patronized by the nobility as well as the riff-raff, all betting heavily, while bear-baiting could be witnessed at 'The Bear-Garden' at Hockey-in-the-Hole.

'The house of the Devil'

The Londoners of Handel's day amused themselves in boisterous ways. It was not until the 1780s that the capital's theatres provided anything like the well-conducted entertainment we are familiar with today. Only when the old custom of allowing members of the audience to sit on the stage was stopped in 1762

done thing to attend the chapel at Magdalen Hospital (in fact, many now famous hospitals were founded in the Georgian era, notably Guy's, the Foundling and St. Thomas's).

The Established Church was in a very complacent state and Protestant dissenters and Catholics were excluded from the universities as well as many public offices unless they paid allegiance to it. Many Anglican bishops carried out few pastoral duties, preferring to dispense favours and patronage, and living richly, while the over-worked lower clergy suffered. Secure in its monopoly, this Established Church upheld a bland and unquestioning view of Christianity and in such circumstances it was not surprising that the most important religious movement of the 18th century was the evangelical revival led by John Wesley (1703–91).

The London of Handel's day was a city of extreme contrasts, a true metropolis where squalor and magnificence, poverty and wealth, cynicism and piety, violence and *joie de vivre* all jostled alongside one another. It was a city which could not be ignored and which aroused strong feelings, such as the often repeated opinion of Dr Johnson, who declared that 'when a man is tired of London, he is tired of life; for there is in London all that life can afford'.

The contempt Hogarth felt for the Established Church can be seen clearly in his 'Sleeping Congregation' (below), where he fiercely ridicules the apathetic and lackadaisical attitudes of both clergy and congregation alike. Like many other Londoners, however, he was relatively unimpressed with the evangelical fervour of John Wesley (left) that was gaining popularity in other parts of Britain.

did the 'house of the Devil' even begin to be more respectable. Even so, few people stayed for the whole evening; many attended only to make assignations with lovers or prostitutes. Audiences rarely went to see one play or concert: they also expected a farce, a pantomime, a ballet and some music. But opera was more exclusive. Most music was written by foreigners who, although living in London remained foreign; only Handel was considered to be a Londoner.

The best shops in 18th-century London were scattered far and wide across the capital, though certain trades still congregated in particular districts. Apart from some luxury shops in Bond Street and St James's, there were no shopping streets as such and many shops were still in the City. The rich went to George Seddon for furniture and mirrors; to Henry Clay for *papier mâché,* and old book shops (often also publishing houses) were still in St Paul's Churchyard and Fleet Street, though new ones gradually opened in Pall Mall and Piccadilly. There were goldsmiths in Cranbourne Street and perfumiers in Shire Lane and it was smart to eat strawberries at Netty's Fruit Shop in St James's Street. Shop-keepers and assistants cringed to the 'carriage trade' and other prestigious customers who were carried from their own front doors to the front door of the shops in silk-lined leather sedan-chairs.

The rise of Methodism

Like entertainments and shopping, religion was also largely a matter of taste and means, and certain churches were deemed more fashionable than others. Thus high society favoured such new churches at St Martin-in-the-Fields (in what is now Trafalgar Square), St Mary-le-Strand and St George's in Hanover Square. And if a famous clergyman such as the Reverend Dodd were preaching there, it was the

IN THE BACKGROUND

The scientific revolution

'Science is the knowledge of consequences, and dependence of one fact upon another', wrote Thomas Hobbes in Leviathan *(1651). This dictum would not have been believed by most people before the 17th century. The authority of the Bible and the teaching of the Churches were absolute, and those who sought to question them risked censure, imprisonment or even death. The development of humanist thought during the Renaissance and the discovery of previously unknown lands led to a more enquiring outlook among the educated classes. The excitement over new scientific theories and inventions was not confined to a few scholars; books explaining the new ideas in simple terms were bestsellers, and royal, aristocratic and middle-class families alike took up scientific study as the latest fashion.*

Old methods of thought did not die out immediately: Sir Isaac Newton himself regarded his alchemical studies as being as important as his mathematical writings, and only later did scientific method dominate educated thought.

IN THE BACKGROUND
'All was light!'

As Handel's days drew to an end, a new age that had its roots in his early lifetime was beginning to emerge – the age of science. This burgeoning age was to change the old-style world for ever.

The birth of modern science came about through an explosion of inventive thought and inspired questioning that spanned two revolutionary centuries and cast aside the long-standing but blinkered world view imposed by scripture and the classics. At the beginning of the 17th century the authority of the Bible was absolute and its literal interpretation was the daily preoccupation of most scholars. Even the rich 'scientific' legacy of the Greek and Roman classics was thought to reflect no more than some 'divine' purpose.

According to these authorities, the Earth was the centre of the universe and, as the only rational beings on the only inhabited planet, the entire cosmos centred upon man. Everyday misfortunes were seen as the work of divine or demonic forces and such

The wonders of the age of science captured the popular imagination. Here, a family gathers round an orrery – a clockwork model of the universe.

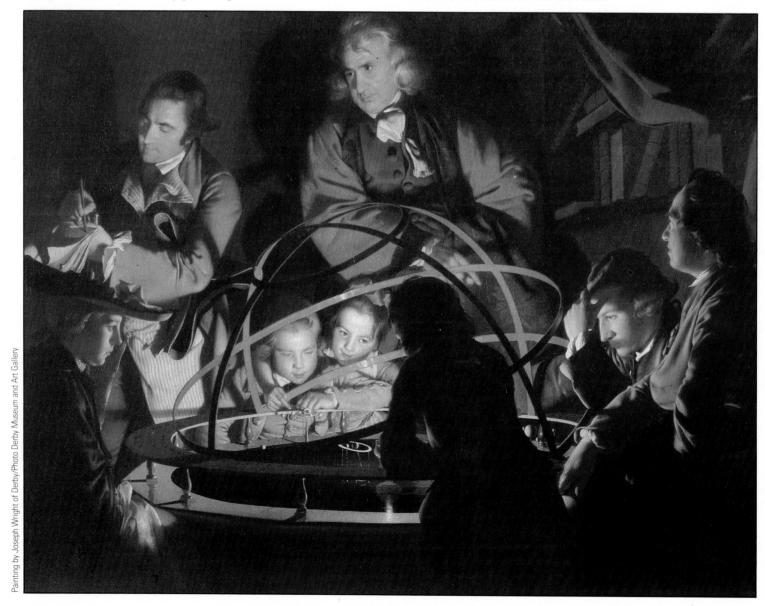

PHILOSOPHIÆ
NATURALIS
PRINCIPIA
᛫MATHEMATICA᛫

Autore *J S. NEWTON,* Trin. Coll. Cantab. Soc. Mathefec᛫
Profeffore *Lucafiano,* & Societatis Regalis Sodali.

IMPRIMATUR᛫
S. P E P Y S, *Reg. Soc.* P R Æ S E S.
Julii 5. 1686.

A leading figure of the scientific revolution was Sir Isaac Newton (far left). In his work Principia Mathematica (left) he laid down a set of physical laws to back up his theory of gravitation. He thereby took astronomy out of the realms of theology by proving his points with precise mathematical calculations.

disasters as the Black Death seemed to be caused by the wrath of God.

In such a climate, it is hardly surprising that the 16th and 17th centuries were times of hysterical witchcraft trials and that, in these times too, the shadow of the Spanish Inquisition fell across Europe. Natural phenomena were explained only in terms of some ultimate will and direction that transcended all scientific enquiry. Science, in so far as it was studied at all, was no more than a branch of theology and philosophy. It was, however, the gradual rejection of these ideas and the glimmering light cast by tentative new discoveries and philosophies that showed the way for an all-consuming scientific revolution.

It is difficult today to fully appreciate the fervent excitement and curiosity that seemed to take hold of western society at the end of the 17th century and maintained its grip throughout the 18th. Popular science books, like Buffon's *Natural History* (1749–1788) and *Newtonianism for Ladies* were such successful best sellers that they ran to numerous reprints. Fashionable people everywhere took up scientific observation and experiment as a leisure activity. While one person started, say, a butterfly collection, another might be getting together an album containing every known kind of plant. Next door, the neighbours might have ordered a set of prisms, in order to experiment with rays of light, while the cultivated Romeo down the road was dispatching to his lady-love a surprise package of rare insects!

Even royalty caught the infection and, throughout the drawing rooms and salons of western Europe, new scientific papers and the latest ideas were eagerly – and intelligently – discussed. Laboratories, botanical gardens and menageries of exotic animals were added to aristocratic mansions and the newest inventions, like the microscope and telescope, were produced in their thousands for a seemingly insatiable market.

No single factor brought about the extraordinary sequence of discoveries made in the 17th century, though various important events did have particular significance. Oceanic explorations, from the 15th century onwards, created pressing new demands on the ancient disciplines of astronomy and mathematics and more accurate navigational instruments were demanded. The discovery of the New World in turn led to the introduction of new plants, animals and peoples to Europe. The heady excitement and ultimately unsettling effects of these voyages stimulated scientific observation and experiment and provided an appropriate setting for the pioneering work of three outstanding individuals.

Prophets of the revolution

The 'father of science' in England was the scientist, politician and essayist Francis Bacon (1561–1626). He made no stupendous scientific discoveries (in fact his scientific knowledge was in many ways old-fashioned) but his philosophical ideas gave a tremendous impetus to future scientific thought. He

By the late 17th century the study of science was breaking new ground. Voyages of exploration and new discoveries had Western society bubbling over with excitement and curiosity. People on their travels spread the word and with the aid of new scientific instruments, such as the telescope, were able to study natural phenomena. The group of Europeans in the painting below are studying the eclipse of the sun in Siam, 1688.

ordinary instrument, he observed the satellites of Jupiter, the valleys of the moon, spots on the sun and even the distant clusters of stars that made up the Milky Way. He also proved that the earth revolved around the sun (a theory first put forward by the Polish astronomer, Copernicus, in 1543) in contradiction to the prevailing Church teaching that the earth was a stationary planet.

Another of Galileo's inventions came about through simple but scientific observation. The story goes that, while he was still a student of Pisa University, Galileo happened to be inside Pisa Cathedral when an earthquake shook the city. One of the suspended lamps started to swing back and forth and Galileo used his own pulse-rate to time the swings. He found that, even when they grew bigger, the oscillations always took exactly the same length of time; the pendulum clock had been born.

Galileo recklessly set down his views and observations in defiance of a papal command and his *Dialogues on the Two Chief Systems of the World* was published in 1632. He dedicated the book to the

Keen to encourage the development of science, Charles II founded the Royal Society in 1662 – only two years after his return from exile.

rejected the authority of traditional wisdom in all branches of learning and believed that only by experiment and induction (testing a hypothesis by facts) could the truth be uncovered. His great contribution was, therefore, his insistence that knowledge was the fruit of experiment. The French encyclopedist Diderot described Bacon as an 'extraordinary genius' who 'when it was impossible to write a history of what men knew, wrote the outline of what men had yet to learn'.

Another founding-father, and near contemporary of Bacon's, was Réné Descartes (1596–1650), the 'father of modern philosophy'. Descartes emphasised the need to use mathematical reasoning and constant doubt as tools of scientific and philosophical inquiry. Though it seems obvious to modern scholars, his great innovation was to believe nothing until it had been proved. Both Descartes and Bacon separated science from theology and both passionately believed that science could and must be used to improve man's lot in life.

The major role of innovator, however, belongs to Galilei Galileo, the brilliant Italian astronomer-mathematician who was arguably the first natural scientist. Taking up the idea that God had given man two 'books' – the Bible and Nature – Galileo insisted that the language of nature was mathematics. His analytical method was composed of three stages; rational intuition, laboratory experiment and mathematical demonstration. He thus united actual observations of the life around him with clinical calculation. No less important, however, was his astronomical work. In the spring of 1609, he learned of the recent invention of the telescope (by a Dutch spectacle-maker named Hans Lippershey). Building models for himself and making improvements as he went along, Galileo produced a telescope that could give a magnification of 32 times. Using this extra-

To believe nothing until it has been proved was the philosophy behind the work of the great mathematician and metaphysician, Réné Descartes. The painting (right) shows Descartes in discourse with Queen Christina of Sweden at Stockholm.

Pope, but this act of courtesy did him little good. The work was greeted with acclaim by scholars throughout Europe, but its author was seized by the Inquisition and, under threat of torture, forced to recant his ideas. Few educated Italians seem to have believed the recantation, however, and the story circulated that when Galileo swore his belief that the earth stood still, he whispered under his breath 'eppure si muove (nevertheless it moves).' The Inquisition, too, was not entirely satisfied and Galileo spent the last eight years of his life under house arrest. The fate of this ageing and deeply religious man illustrates just how hard-won was the scientific freedom of the early 17th century.

New scientific instruments

As the 17th century progressed, men of science stopped asking *why* things happened and started to concentrate on *how*. As a result, they started making their own instruments – either by adapting old, familiar tools to new uses or by inventing their own. In a century that began roughly with Galileo and ended with Isaac Newton, the telescope, microscope, pendulum clock, barometer and thermometer were invented. Their impact was immediate for, although there was much progress towards precision, there was often a lack of any standard measure for scientific data. As the development of the thermometer alone shows, the consequence of individual efforts to overcome this problem are still with us today.

Among his many achievements, Galileo is believed to have made an air thermometer – a crude ancestor of the thermometer and barometer. Decisive steps in their further development were taken by Daniel Gabriel Fahrenheit (1686–1736), a leading instrument-maker from Amsterdam. He developed a mercury thermometer to help him determine the boiling points of various different liquids. With zero fixed at the temperature of a given mixture of ice, water and salt, and with the body temperature arbitrarily fixed

A draper by trade and a brilliant microscopist by inclination – Anton van Leeuwenhoek (above) taught himself to grind lenses, and using his own style of microscope (right) made some of the most significant advances of the century in biology.

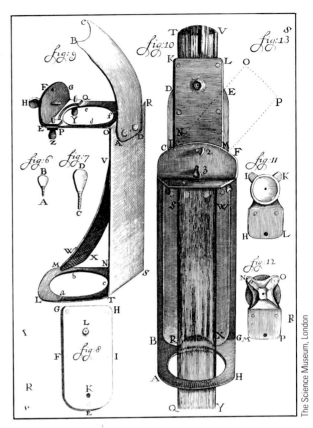

at 96°, Fahrenheit found that the freezing point of water was 32°, and its boiling point was 212°. In Sweden, Anders Celsius (1701–1744) developed a measure of his own – but with a different scale. He put the temperature of melting snow at 100 and of boiling water at zero. With variations introduced in the mid-18th century (including the reversal of the Celsius scale), this thermometer, like Fahrenheit's, is still in use today.

From advances in scientific theory and discovery came the first great steps in practical mechanics. Machinery on a scale never before seen began to be introduced, changing the face of 17th-century Europe. The scene (left) shows a massive machine constructed to transport water from the river to Marly reservoir near Versailles. Fourteen wheels, turned by the flow of the river, worked a tiered system of pumps – 225 in all – which raised the water.

Madame de Pompadour, mistress of Louis XV embraced the spirit of the Age of Reason. For many educated men and women of the time dabbling in 'salon science' was a favourite pastime.

Precision navigational instruments were also developed at this time – in response to the needs of the great voyages of discovery. A high point was the invention of the chronometer (c. 1761), by John Harrison, which made possible the accurate calculation of longitude (based on the difference in time between shipboard and zero meridian). The British government had offered a massive cash prize of £20,000 for the invention of just such a device, and set up a Board of Longitude to oversee its control.

Sadly, Harrison had to fight long and hard for his prize, and eventually gave up after receiving only half the promised amount. Justice was eventually done, however. In 1772, Harrison and his son were granted an audience with King George III – an avid patron of the sciences. When the shameful story was told, the king exclaimed angrily 'By God, Harrison, I'll see you righted' and, under royal pressure, the Board finally paid up!

The new philosophy

By the beginning of the 18th century, the educated man, although a good Christian, was at liberty to openly reject the traditional Biblical view of nature. This radical approach – started by Galileo, Descartes and Francis Bacon – meant that Nature was now treated as a phenomenon devoid of spiritual or human qualities. It could not be understood by a study of the Bible, or of classical writing, but by careful observation and experiment. The human body was now regarded as being mechanical, an important and far-reaching concept in the 17th century. Its influence led to one of the most significant discoveries of all – that of the circulation of blood. The English physiologist, William Harvey (1578–1657) announced this sensational observation in his tract, *De Motu Cordis,* in 1628 and its description of a pump-like heart and the mechanical flow of blood had a profound effect on both medical and philosophical thinking. A growing breed of scientists adopted this new philosophy and, by the end of the century, they had created a new kind of science.

Perhaps the most remarkable feature of a remarkable age, however, was the free interchange of ideas and the spirit of co-operation that existed between scientists and scholars. This sprang from the conviction that scientific progress could not fail to benefit mankind – an optimistic view which persists to this day.

A direct outcome of this ideal was the establishment of eminent scientific societies. From the outset, it was recognized that such societies and their journals must provide a meeting place for the best minds in the land, so that ultimately the results of their combined investigations could be used for the good of the community. Inspired by this spirit, the Royal Society in London was founded in 1662, the French Academie des Sciences in 1666 and the Societas

'Why?' was the single most important question in the age of science, and was the word which drove people on to the road to discovery. Looking back, it gave rise to many bizarre, even amusing, experiments. The group (left) is shown experimenting with the then new and very mysterious power of electricity.

Exploration and discovery in the 18th century broadened many horizons – not the least of which was the attitude to learning. The study of botany became an increasingly popular hobby. The Botanical Gardens at Kew (left) were set up by Princess Augusta in 1759 and later (as shown here) did much to promote the public interest in the strange flora from foreign lands.

Taking a look at an early laboratory (left) gives clues to the many different areas in which 'amateur' scientists dabbled. The quest for knowledge was such that many people tackled a variety of fields rather than simply specializing in one.

Regia Scientiarium (later the Prussian Academy) in 1700. These societies provided libraries, laboratories, stipends and instruments for their members and served as a national clearing house for both the scientist and the amateur scholar. Thanks to their efforts, communication between scientists around Europe was both easy and productive. The traditional hot-houses of learning, the universities, were with very few exceptions (such as the University of Padua and the University of Leiden) still locked into out-dated methods and surprisingly contributed very little to scientific progress.

Sir Isaac Newton

Even with all its great luminaries, the scientific revolution was dominated by the figure of Sir Isaac Newton – one of the outstanding scientists and mathematicians of all time. Albert Einstein said of his work that it was 'perhaps the greatest intellectual stride that it has been granted to any man to make'. Newton's epoch-making contributions included the foundation of the differential and integral calculus and the analysis of light and optics. His best-known discovery, traditionally inspired by the sight of a falling apple, was the conception of a force of gravitation extending from the earth to the moon. He published details of the theory in his masterpiece, *Principia Mathematica* (1687). This work was, in many ways, the result of advances made during the two preceding centuries and it owed much to the researches of Leonardo da Vinci, Kepler, Galileo, Hooke and Halley. It was, however, Newton who produced the final proofs of their theories and in so

Scientific Researches! — New Discoveries in PNEUMATICS! — or — an Experimental Lecture o Powers of Air

Inevitably, new discoveries were greeted with a certain degree of scepticism, and their mesmeric hold on the public was often mocked (above).

doing, created a picture of the universe as a rigid mechanism held together by absolute mechanical laws, founded on the principle of gravitation.

The *Principia* immediately raised Newton to international stardom. Although only a handful of people really understood the complexity of his thinking, the work was a triumphant and inspiring example of the possibilities of the new learning. The tremendous impact of his work is best summed up in the famous lines by Alexander Pope:

Nature and Nature's laws lay hid by night,
God said, let Newton be! and all was light.

His fame spread steadily and scientists around the world set about trying to test his theories. But it was not just the experts who became obsessed: one observer noted that 'barristers neglect the Bar, clerics their theological exercises, all for the sake of finding out about the Law of Gravitation'.

Yet many of the contradictions inherent in the scientific revolution are exemplified by Newton. Scientific rivalry existed side by side with the spirit of co-operation. Newton engaged in particularly ugly disputes with first Robert Hooke and later Leibnitz, the German philosopher and mathematician. His tyrannical rule over the Royal Society would brook no hint of criticism of his own work, while he actively victimized the Astronomer Royal, John Flamsteed. Deeply interested in religion and philosophy, Newton devoted much of his later life to the interpretation of the prophecies of Daniel and St John. Paradoxically, we find him struggling to discover the exact plan of Solomon's temple — because he considered it the best guide to the topography of heaven! It seems extraordinary that a man whose observation and experiment revealed so much of the natural world could, at the same time, be so obsessed with the old-fashioned and literal interpretation of the Bible.

Advances in biology

The advances in all fields of science were formidable. In 1757, the French scientist Guettard realized that the hills of the Pûy de Dome area were volcanoes that must have become extinct in the very distant past and long before either legend of history could record their existence. Buffon, in his *Theory of the Earth* (1749) and *Epochs of Nature* (1778) reckoned that the earth must be at least 80,000 years old — far in excess of the traditionally accepted age of 6000 years! However, it was not until Charles Lyall published *The Principles of Geology* in three volumes (1830–33) and Charles Darwin his *On the Origin of Species* (1859) that most educated men, including most churchmen, came to accept that the earth was vastly older than once thought.

While such advances were significant, it was in biology that some of the most exciting and astonishing discoveries were made. The path was laid by the Dutch microscopist, Anton van Leeuwenhoek — the first man to observe bacteria, protozoa and spermatozoa through a lens. With little formal education — he was a draper by trade — he taught himself to grind lenses and, during his lifetime made over 400 of them, some no bigger than a pin head. Using these, Leeuwenhoek was able to observe 'very little animalcules' and to isolate them from their various environments — rainwater, the human mouth and the intestines, for example.

His researches into the life histories of various forms of animal life were extensive. He showed, for example, that the weevils found in granaries did not breed from the wheat itself (a popular notion at that time) but were hatched from insect eggs. He also showed that the flea, a 'minute and despised creature', did not breed spontaneously from sand or dust, but was 'endowed with as great perfection in its kind as any large animal'. He similarly proved that eels were not produced from dew but underwent the normal process of regeneration!

Less dramatic, but by no means less important was the work of Carolus Linnaeus, the Swedish botanist who first classified plants and animals by their genera and species, using the internationally recognized language of Latin. Like many other scholars, he quickly established an international reputation and travelled widely throughout Europe.

The Industrial Revolution

The great surge of discovery and invention in science led in turn to the birth of an industry to produce scientific instruments. Because of this the wheel turned full circle: improved instruments led to greater accuracy and further improvements in science. One of the most important events of this period was, therefore, that after some 3000 years of indifference to one another, science and technology were finally united. One example serves to show just how interdependent the different disciplines had become. The new textile industry sorely needed more efficient steam engines to drive its machinery; the engines needed more accurate machine parts made from steel; steel needed a better process for turning coal into coke and the waste products from this process led to the creation of two entirely new industries — gas and chemicals.

The first breakthrough in this chain of events came with the Scottish engineer, James Watt. In his youth, Watt was a 'mathematical instrument-maker' for the University of Glasgow and, while employed by them, he made a study of steam engines and the properties of steam. His studies resulted, in 1769, in the development of a vastly improved steam pump which he spent years adapting into a fully operational engine for driving machinery.

Just as steam power was coming of age, however, a newcomer was about to be born. In 1748, the

The English chemist, Sir Humphrey Davy (shown on the left giving a lecture at the Surrey Institution in 1809) carried out lengthy experiments on the respiration of gases – on a number of occasions nearly losing his life in the process. In 1815 he investigated fire damp and invented his safety lamp for miners.

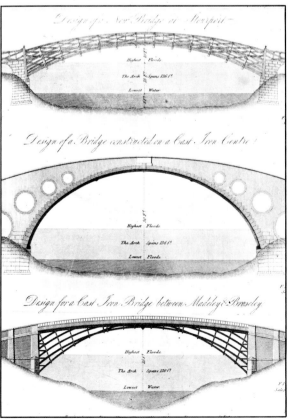

A new technique to smelt iron with coal instead of with charcoal was pioneered in Coalbrookdale, Shropshire, and raised the British iron industry to a number one position. The first iron bridge in the world was built in 1773 in Coalbrookdale – others (left) followed shortly after.

American statesman-scientist Benjamin Franklin, first suggested that electric charges existed in two states, positive and negative. He also proved (by the hazardous method of flying a kite in a thunderstorm) that lightning was an electrical force. From this point onwards, discoveries about electricity followed fast and furious – Volta invented the first battery and Ampère showed that an electric current could produce magnetism. By 1821, a young blacksmith's son, Michael Faraday, had made the very first, if rather crude electric motor and the world had a new source of power.

But the driving force behind all this invention remained coal, and the mines themselves were the key to yet another scientific revolution – the railway. Steam engines designed to haul wagon-loads of ore were the prototypes of locomotives. In 1804, an historical event took place in Merthyr Tydfil, Wales. The locomotive, Catch-me-who-can, hauled a total of five wagons, loaded variously with coal and with 70 extremely nervous passengers; it reached the earth-shattering speed of five miles an hour!

Other industries made contributions in their own right. For example, the English potter and social reformer, Josiah Wedgwood, combined with physicians to pursue research, to form local societies and to patronize scientists. Research was fostered in new and reformed universities and, by the 19th century, scientific inquiry had been taken from the hands of the gentlemen-scholars and had become organized and rigorous. The modern age of science had begun.

Contemporary composers

John Blow
(1649-1708)

Born in London, Blow became a chorister at the Chapel Royal on the Restoration of Charles II in 1660, rising to become organist of Westminster Abbey in 1668 and a Gentleman of the Chapel Royal in 1674. Giving up his Westminster Abbey post for his favourite former pupil, Purcell, Blow was later made Composer to the Chapel Royal. He composed much church music, but had less success with secular works such as his opera *Venus and Adonis*. His *Ode on the Death of Mr. Henry Purcell*, however, is considered masterly.

Giovanni Bononcini
(1670-1747)

Born in Modena, Italy, Bononcini came from a family of musicians and composers. He was a child prodigy, being appointed *maestro di cappella* in Bologna in 1687; and by the age of 21 he had published a great deal of music, including oratorios. Further successes led to a very well-paid appointment at the Viennese court. In 1720 he joined the Royal Academy of Music in London as one of its resident composers. In London his operas, such as *Griselda,* rivalled Handel's in popularity and he was supported by the nobility. But in 1731 Bononcini was found to have passed off someone else's composition as his own and he left England. The Empress Maria Theresa of Austria granted him a small pension. He died in Vienna.

Giacomo Carissimi
(1605-74)

The youngest child of a cooper, Carissimi became *maestro di cappella* at Assisi Cathedral in 1628, but left to take up the same position at the German College of the Jesuit Order in Rome, where he remained for the rest of his life. He is renowned for his religions dialogues and oratorios, based for the most part on Old Testament themes, such as *Jonas*. He also wrote over 100 cantatas, adopting Monteverdi's idiom to sacred texts. The German College attracted many pupils while he was there. He died in Rome.

François Couperin
(1668-1733)

Born in Paris to a family of musicians – who, unlike the Bach's, remained in their native country – Couperin was taught by his father, who had influence at court. In 1693 he was made one of the four court organists and in 1696 ennobled. Over the next years he composed chamber music for the courtly Sunday concerts. In 1713 he began publishing the music which has made him famous – the suites for harpsichord, in four books, 1713–30. Called *ordres,* most are in dance rhythms, usually with titles. Some are portraits of friends, as in Elgar's *Enigma Variations.* Rarely passionate yet keenly felt, Couperin's music is sometimes compared with Watteau's painting. His later years were marred by ill health. He died in Paris.

Jean Baptiste Lully
(1632-87)

The son of a miller in Florence, he was taken to France in 1646 where he became famous for his skills as a violinist. In 1653 he was made *compositeur de la musique instrumentale* to Louis XIV, in whose service he then remained for the rest of his life. In the 1660s he wrote many ballets, much incidental music and – in 1672 – *Cadmus et Hermione,* the first of 10 *tragedies lyriques.* He died of gangrene contracted from striking his foot with his cane while conducting his great *Te Deum* before the king. Although he trained the finest orchestra in Europe's premier court, he was essentially a restrictive and unenterprising composer.

Domenico Scarlatti
(1685-1757)

Born in Naples, where his father Alessandro was *maestro di cappella* to the Viceroy, Scarlatti was appointed organist to the royal chapel at the age of 15. Until his late 20s he was oppressed by his father's overbearing influence, his work up to 1719 being mere pale imitations of his parent's. In that year, however, he left Italy for Portugal, where he became harpsichord teacher to the Infanta Maria Barbara. When she married the Spanish Crown Prince in 1728, Scarlatti also moved to Madrid, where he died. Scarlatti wrote over 500, still famous, harpsichord sonatas for his royal pupil.

Bibliography

G. Abraham, *Handel: A Symposium,* Greenwood, Westport, 1980

W. Cummings, *Purcell,* Haskell, New York, 1969

A. Davison, *Bach and Handel: The Consummation of the Baroque in Music,* Da Capo, New York, 1986

W. Dean, *Handel's Dramatic Oratorios and Masques,* Oxford University Press, Oxford, 1959

H. Eggebrecht, 'Johann Pachelbel als Vokalkomponnist', *Arkiv für Musikwissenschaft* XI, 1954

J. Engels, *Vivaldi in Early Fall,* University of Georgia Press, Athens, 1982

A. Hutchings, *Purcell,* University of Washington Press, Seattle, 1983

A. Hutchings, *The Baroque Concerto,* Faber and Faber, London, 1961

J. Keates, *Handel: The Man and His Music,* St. Martins Press, New York, 1985

W. Kolneder, *Antonio Vivaldi: His Life and Work,* Faber and Faber, London, 1974

R. Myers, *Handel's Messiah: A Touchstone of Taste,* Hippocrene Books, New York, 1971

M. Pincherle, *Vivaldi: Genius of the Baroque,* Norton Press, New York, 1962

M. Pincherle, *Corelli: His life and his Music,* Da Capo, New York, 1979

P. Robinson, *Handel and His Orbit,* Da Capo, New York, 1979

S. Sadie, *Handel,* Riverrun, New York, 1981

S. Sadie, *Handel Concertos,* University of Washington Press, Seattle, 1973

R. Streatfield, *Handel,* Greenwood, Westport, 1978

M. Talbot, *Vivaldi,* J. M. Dent, London, 1984

M. Talbot, 'Albinoni: The Professional Dilettante', *The Musical Times,* CXIII, London, 1971

R. Walker, 'Rameau, Rousseau and the "Essaie sur l'origine des langues"', 'Studies in Voltaire and the 18th Century, vol. 117, London, 1974

P. Williams, *Bach, Handel and Scarlatti: Tercentenary Essays,* Cambridge Univerity Press, Cambridge, 1985

P. Young, *Handel,* J. M. Dent, London, 1947

F. Zimmerman, *Henry Purcell 1659-95: His Life and Times,* St. Martins Press, New York, 1967

Index